An Elizabethan Alphabet

the fifth book in the Elizabethan Needlework Series

GPL **GEORGESON PUBLISHING LIMITED**

by Shirley Paulin

Embroidery threads used throughout this book were supplied by Warnaar Trading Company Limited.

Published by Georgeson Publishing Limited
P.O. Box 100-667
North Shore Mail Centre, Auckland
New Zealand
Ph: 649 410 2079 Fax: 649 410 2069
Email: gpl@georgeson.co.nz Web site: www.georgeson.co.nz

We have made every effort to ensure that these instructions are accurate and complete. We cannot, however, be responsible for human error, typographical mistakes or variations in individual work.

ISBN No. 0-9582105-1-9

Editor: Prue Georgeson
Photography: Maria Sainsbury
Illustrations: Shirley Paulin
Stitch Diagrams and Layout: Andreena Buckton, Noodle Design Corp.
Printed in New Zealand

Contents

AN ELIZABETHAN ALPHABET
INTRODUCTION

I was born and brought up on our family farm in the small country village of Becks in Central Otago. My mother was a great needlewoman and many of her pieces decorated our family home. My earliest memory of stitching was making an oven cloth using a sugar bag with threads withdrawn and the cross stitch worked with pure wool in clear bright colours. My interest in embroidery continued at secondary school and as a young adult, evening classes with the highly respected tutor, the late Miss Helen Moran, continued to foster this interest.

After marriage, to Pat a school teacher, I lived in a number of small South Island towns and there was less time for my embroidery. It was not until our return to the city of Dunedin that I could resume embroidery classes. A class with the author of *Exploring Elizabethan Embroidery*, the late Dorothy Clarke proved an inspiration and I decided to embroider our five grandchildren's names, Blake, Joshua, Bradley, Hope and Heath using Elizabethan stitching techniques.

The children wanted all the flowers, fruit and creatures that I could possibly fit in around their names so this is what I did. They have proved a very popular 'heirloom' for the children and their mothers Sharon and Debbie. I hope you will enjoy many happy hours stitching in this technique, chose letters from my alphabet and flowers, fruit and creatures that inhabit these pages to create your own unique design. It will be a very special gift for the chosen recipient.
Enjoy these wonderful techniques and become a creative embroiderer and surprise your family and friends. As my 5 year old grandson says 'Nanny anything is possible when you use your imagination'.

Shirley Paulin 2001

HOW TO USE THIS BOOK

A LITTLE BACKGROUND INFORMATION BEFORE YOU START

This book has been written for embroiderers new to embroidery in the style of Elizabethan Coloured Silk Embroidery or for those who have tried this technique and would like new designs. *Exploring Elizabethan Embroidery* by Dorothy Clarke with designs by Stephanie Powell is the first book in the *Elizabethan Needlework Series* and may be used in conjunction with this book. More advanced designs may be found in *Elizabethan Needlework Accessories* and *Festive Elizabethan Creations* with designs for Christmas in *An Elizabethan Christmas*.

The evolution of the alphabet involved two major steps forward, firstly the invention of a writing system that expressed the sound of consonants in our daily language (between 1700 and 1500BC) and secondly, the invention of characters for representing vowels (between 800 - 700 BC). Forms of written language then developed along many different avenues[1]. The alphabet used in English has developed over the centuries and as recently as 1800 was different from the alphabet we know today in that I and J and U and V were not given separate listings in English dictionaries until the publication of Webster in 1828[2]. Spoken English has also changed over the centuries with the usage and spelling of Chaucer's time being quite different to that used by the Elizabethans whose language in turn would barely be understood today.

English in the Elizabethan times was not a standard language. Rather there was a huge diversity of speech with many different dialects. However there was a movement at the time towards "establishing a standard English, the speech of the court and the educated classes of London and about sixty miles round, thus including the universities"[3]. The movement to reform spelling was supported by the advantage this would have for trade as well as for teaching foreigners the language. By the later years of Elizabeth's reign people of learning were starting to write their works in English to "benefit their countrymen rather than publishing in Latin to purchase fame among strangers"[4]. Latin being the traditional language of learning at that time.

The letters of the alphabet lend themselves to decoration. Medieval manuscripts have exquisitely decorated pages in which each letter is a work of art. Needlewomen have long enjoyed decorating letters in a wide variety of different stitching techniques. Possibly the most widely known use is in the alphabets stitched on samplers which varied from the very simple alphabets found on marking samplers to the elaborate and decorated letters found on Dutch and Scottish Samplers in particular.

An Elizabethan Alphabet continues the tradition of decorating text. Each letter of the alphabet is decorated with flowers, birds, animals or insects stitched in the techniques used by Elizabethan embroiderers' in coloured silk embroidery, one of the very popular techniques of that day. Suggestions are given for ways of combining the letters of the alphabet with the different flora and fauna to create unique designs for the special people in your life.

The stitches are not hard, the main filling stitch being a variation of buttonhole stitch, plus other useful surface stitches, all of which are shown in clear, easy-to-follow diagrams with accompanying text.

The special joy of this embroidery is the colour and texture achieved in the designs which make them very enticing and enjoyable to stitch. The threads used are Perle 8, Coton a broder 16, or threads of a similar weight which are slightly heavier than the stranded cottons we all know so well. These threads help to develop the texture for which this stitchery is known and loved.

FOOTNOTES

1.   A useful general reference being www.britannica.com
2.   Sampler and Antique Needlework Quarterly, Fall 2000 page 33.
3.   The ElizabethanRenaissance, The Cultural Achievement, A.L. Rowse, MacMillan London 1972
4.   The ElizabethanRenaissance, The Cultural Achievement, A.L. Rowse, MacMillan London 1972
5.   The Alphabetic Labyrinth, Johanna Drucker, Thames and Hudson, London, 1995.

REQUIREMENTS

FABRIC

This embroidery is best stitched on a firm, closely-woven fabric e.g. linen, furnishing fabric, closely woven sheeting or satin. The designs in this book have been stitched on a variety of different fabrics. When choosing a fabric (background) select one that compliments the foreground e.g. a wedding accessory that is complimentary to the gowns being worn, fabric a colour to suit a child's room. To give the fabric additional strength, required because this embroidery is all on the surface and because it is very textured, the use of 'Stayflex' or any iron-on fabric interlining is recommended. Transfer the design to the fabric first, then iron-on the fabric interlining of your choice before starting to stitch.

THREADS TO USE

The threads used mainly are DMC Perle 8 and Coton a broder 16 and these two may be used interchangeably. At your local needlework store you may find other threads of a similar weight which could also be used. Perle 8 is approximately equivalent to three threads of stranded cotton and I have used this in places where the colour I wanted was not available in Coton a Broder or Perle 8. Avoid stranded threads if possible as they tend to separate and it is harder to achieve a neat finished result. Random or overdyed threads may also be used and would give beautiful shading in a design. Use familiar threads or experiment with new ones to expand your skills.

Metallic threads can be used in the needle with another thread and stitched as one, or used to stitch highlights in your design.

NEEDLES

This embroidery is worked using No.8 crewel needles, No. 24 or 26 tapestry needles and No. 10-13 beading needles or No. 10 straw needles. The crewel needle has a long eye and a sharp point and is used to work stitches which pierce the ground fabric. The tapestry needle has a long eye but a blunt tip and is used for detached buttonhole stitching. The beading or straw needles are long and fine and are used to stitch the beads to the embroidery.

EMBELLISHMENT

Embellish with beads wherever there is a gap or to make the design more pleasing and visually interesting.

SCISSORS

There are many different types of scissors available. For this embroidery a blunt-nosed pair which can be used to push dacron inside shapes and snip the odd thread are what is required.

If you feel more comfortable holding your embroidery in a frame you will need either a small circular hoop about 10cms (4") in diameter which can be used to encircle a small area or a hoop large enough to include the entire design. A slate frame could also be used. It is important that the embroidery is not flattened after it is worked when re-positioning the hoop.

EMBROIDERY FRAME -HOOP

This embroidery does not need to be worked in a frame and I do not use a frame myself. The chain stitch which is worked around each shape initially must be worked in the hand as the stitches must be small and they can not be stitched small enough if worked in a frame.

If you feel more comfortable holding your embroidery in a frame you will need either a small circular hoop about 10cms (4") in diameter which can be used to encircle a small area or a hoop large enough to include the entire design. A slate frame could also be used. It is important that the embroidery is not flattened after it is worked when re-positioning the hoop.

EXTRAS

It is useful if you have a little stuffing, or dacron cushion filling to hand ready to push beneath the completed petals, leaves and animals to give the embroidery a raised appearance.

PREPARING THE DESIGN

Trace the letters of the name or initial you wish to use from the alphabet section, Mono Baking Paper works well.
Cut the letters out and place them on another sheet of paper leaving room for a selection of flora and fauna from the book to be placed around the letters. Allow spaces in the letters for alternative designs e.g. flowers, bugs, or fruits to be placed on the outline of the letters as in 'K' page 48. The flora and fauna may also be positioned behind or in front of the letters see the snail which is positioned behind the letter 'B' and the Squirrel which has its tail on top of the 'B' in Blake page 55.

Trace the flora and fauna designs you like, then cut out and place them around and on the letters you plan to embroider until you achieve a design you are happy with. You will see that the embroidered names I stitched for my grandchildren pages 54 - 55 have a large number of designs embroidered on them, this was because my grandchildren particularly wanted them. For 'Sara' page 49 'Emma' page 53 and the Christmas Design 'Noel' page 56. I chose fewer designs so that the letters stood out very clearly - this is a personal decision, be guided by your own and the recipient's preference.

You will notice that some of the designs for the flora and fauna which appear on the embroidery created for my grandchildren are not shown in this book. The designs for these are to be found in *Exploring Elizabethan Embroidery* by Dorothy Clarke. Once you have stitched some of my designs you will have the skills to include in your stitching other animals birds or flowers of particular significance to you or the recipient.

There are many different ways to link each letter. On each page featuring a letter from the alphabet you will see that I give suggestions for how to link this letter with another. It is not possible to cover every possible combination of letters, these are given as a guide only.

If the name you wish to embroider is particularly long, you may wish to place the letters closer together than I have or to stitch the letters, apart from the first, in lower case as I did in 'Anne' and surround the name with a border of flowers birds and animals. Smaller flora and fauna can be placed on lower case letters. There are many alphabets available and you may wish to use a personal favourite, this technique encourages experimentation and creativity.

When you have created a pleasing arrangement place a further sheet of paper over the whole design area, trace the design to this and transfer it to the linen using your preferred method.

TO TRANSFER THE DESIGN

Fold the paper with your design traced onto it in half to find the centre and likewise fold the linen to establish the centre. Transfer the design on to your fabric. I suggest outlining the design in black and then tracing using a lightbox, (a lamp under a glass table works in the same way), or alternatively tape the design to the window, put your fabric over the design and then transfer the design to the fabric. Trace with a very sharp soft lead 6B pencil. You may prefer to use Sewing Carbon paper. *Trace the main outlines only*, do not transfer any fine details e.g. a spiders web, the feelers on the bee or caterpillar etc as they may not be hidden by subsequent stitching

Sometimes I tack the design on if the fabric is very delicate or conversely if the fabric is coarse and can't be traced through. To transfer by tacking again trace only the main outlines of the design onto white tissue paper. Lay the paper over the area to be worked, pin or tack in place before tacking the design outline using light coloured sewing machine cotton and small stitches. The design outline may also be tacked with the sewing machine using large stitches. Once the design outline is tacked to your fabric, remove the tissue paper.

Iron on backing fabric before you start to stitch

COLOURS

Colour choices are extremely personal, when selecting threads for your own designs you may be influenced by the colour scheme of the room the embroidery will be placed in, or the favourite colour of the person the embroidery is for. The linen selected for the design will influence the choice of threads to be used on it for both the lettering and the flora and fauna. Traditional reds always look good for Christmas, creams and white for a wedding and pastels for baby. If you are ever unsure of the colours to use look no further than the colours used in nature for flowers, birds, and animals and your embroidery will always look attractive.

For lettering I personally recommend choosing a bold, bright colour to achieve impact and create an irresistible 'carnival of colour' for the flowers and fauna.

Finishing or 'Blocking'

This embroidery is not completed until you have embroidered the date of its completion and your name on a corner of the linen. It may last hundreds of years and a date and your name will give it extra value and interest in the years ahead.

This embroidery must not be ironed when it is completed. If ironed it will lose the rich texture you have created with your surface stitchery and padding.

Method

Take the soft pinex board and place the 1 cm (1/2") grid graph paper on top of the board. Then cover the whole board and graph paper with the waterproof acetate. It is extremely important that the dampness from your embroidery cannot get through to the pinex board as this could stain your embroidery.

Now completely soak your embroidery by gently washing it in a mild soap (Lux or Sunlight) and then stretch it out onto the board, right side facing up, placing the top of the material along a line on the graph paper, stretch firmly.

Put tacks along the top of the material at 3 to 4cm (1 - 1 1/2") intervals. Now stretch the material down along the left and right hand sides keeping it an equal distance from the nearest line on each side and placing tacks at 3 to 4cm (1 - 1 1/2") intervals. Finally tack along the bottom of the embroidery once again placing tacks at 3 to 4cm (1 - 1 1/2") intervals.

Your work is now 'blocked' and must be left tacked like this until it is completely dry. Blocking removes any puckers or wrinkles and serves as an alternative to ironing which is not suitable with this technique.

Requirements

- Soft pinex board at least 10cm (4") bigger than your embroidery - a cake board or ceiling tile works well.
- Graph paper, preferably about a 1 cm grid - the lines on the graph paper are extremely useful when it comes to stretching your embroidery and keeping it square.
- Waterproof acetate, duraseal, or contact
- Tack pins (for blocking) rust proof preferably.

CHAIN STITCH

actual size 10- 12 stitches per inch

Chain stitch is the most frequently used stitch in Elizabethan embroidery. It is used to outline most shapes worked in the designs in this book and it is always worked first. The chain stitch must be kept small and even as subsequent stitches are worked into the initial chain stitch outline. It is worked using a No. 8 crewel or embroidery needle.

HOW TO STITCH A SHARP POINT IN CHAIN STITCH

In Elizabethan Embroidery further stitches are frequently worked into the chain stitch outline of the shapes so it is most important to be able to work chain stitch to create a nice point. 'Rounded' points on a leaf or calyx would ruin its appearance.

Chain stitch to the point, then take the thread from the chain at the tip of the point through to the back of the work. To anchor the chain do a small back stitch at the back of your work then bring the needle through to the front at the same place you went down and continue chain stitching away from the point. Try to have the two sides of the point with an equal number of stitches up to and away from the point so that you can work subsequent stitches evenly (fig. 2).

fig. 1.

fig. 2.

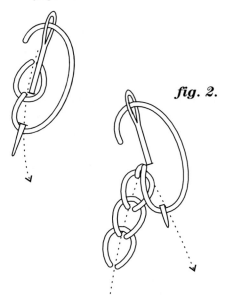

HOW TO CHAIN STITCH A COMPLETE CIRCLE OR AROUND THE OUTLINE OF A SHAPE

Stitch round the circle or shape until you are just one stitch from joining the beginning of the circle then take the needle under both threads of the first chain as shown taking the needle through to the back of the material just beside the point where your thread came out from the last chain in the circle (fig. 3).

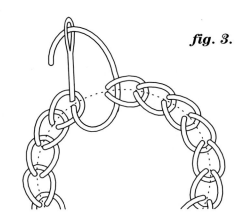

fig. 3.

WHIPPED CHAIN STITCH

WHIPPED CHAIN STITCH

This makes a textured cord like stitch and is a good alternative to ladder stitch for working the letters of the alphabet. Working from right to left with a blunt needle, bring the thread up beside the beginning of the chain then pass the needle under each chain stitch without going through the fabric until the end.

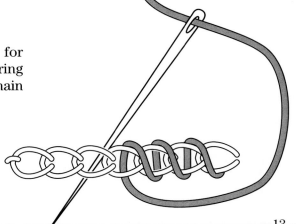

LACED CHAIN

fig. 1.

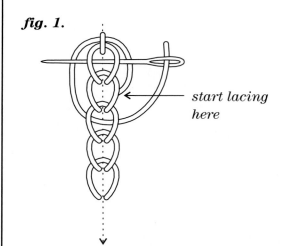

start lacing here

A line of chain stitch is worked finishing with a little straight stitch to anchor the last chain down. With the straight stitch at the top of your work take a thread of a different colour and bring your needle out beside the line of chain stitch two chains down from where you finished. Take the thread up to the straight stitch and thread the needle under the straight stitch, bring the thread down three chains (so that it is now one in front of where you started) and take the thread under the chain.

Now take the thread back up two chain stitches and thread the needle under the chain stitch, bring the thread down three chains and continue as before, gradually working your way down the line of chain stitch. The looped thread can be left as large or small as required depending on the size of the leaf you are working on. When you are ready to finish hold the last loop made, carefully between your finger and thumb, take the needle through to the back of the work beside the last chain stitch and do a back stitch to anchor your thread.

PICOT STITCH

also known as Needlewoven bars

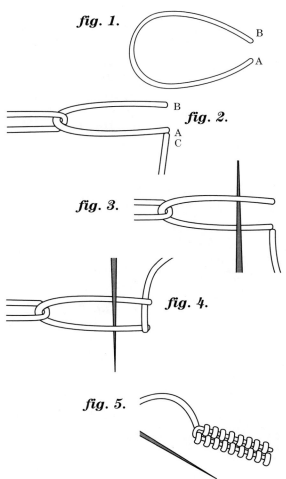

fig. 1.

fig. 2.

fig. 3.

fig. 4.

fig. 5.

This little picot is the perfect way to make three dimensional sepals, little leaves, or petals. The picot can be attached to the fabric at the end or run the thread down the back of the stitching to the background fabric and leave the end unattached.

Catch the thread on the back. Bring the thread to the front at A then take through to the back at B leaving a loop of thread on the front of the material the required length for the sepal, or petal you are making, say 10mm (3/8").

Bring the needle back out at C, just below A taking care not to catch the loop at all. Thread a piece of waste thread through the loop and with your left hand hold the thread taut, slightly above the surface of the work while you stitch.

Weave the needle over the lower thread of the loop and under the upper thread, do not catch the fabric. Pull the thread through and push the thread down close to the fabric with your needle.

Now weave the needle over the upper thread and under the lower thread, again taking care not to catch the fabric. Push the woven thread down firmly so it is snugly against the first wrap

Continue weaving backwards and forward over the two threads until the loop is fully woven, make sure the wraps are packed down firmly. Take out the waste thread. The picot bar may be attached at this end to the background fabric or you may prefer to take the thread down the back of the needleweaving to leave the picot free at one end.

LADDER STITCH

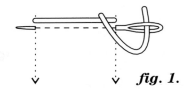

fig. 1.

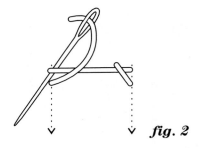

fig. 2

This stitch creates a heavy textured outline and I have used it to stitch all the letters of the alphabet. It also gives an interesting variation for a leaf shape.

It is well worth persevering to master this stitch. You may find working a leaf first is a good way to practise the technique. As the name states there is a space between each rung of a 'ladder'. If the stitches are worked too closely together the line becomes wobbly and an uneven appearance develops. It is hard to work effectively in tight scrolls so for that reason I work very fine tendrils in chain stitch. You may replace ladder stitch with a variety of other stitches, see page 24 for alternatives.

WORKING LADDER STITCH

Step 1 Work a straight stitch first and come up above it on the right hand side as shown. Then take a second straight stitch beneath the first bringing the needle out directly beneath the first stitch (fig.1).

Step 2 Take the needle through the first straight stitch you worked, on the left hand side (not picking up the material, only the thread) as shown (fig. 2). Pull thread firm but not tight.

Step 3 Loop the thread across to the right hand side and pass the needle under the straight stitch and the angled stitch on the right hand side. (Don't pick up the material - just the thread.) Leave the thread a little slack (fig. 3).

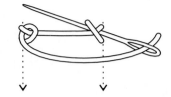

fig. 3.

Step 4 Now take the needle through the fabric from right to left as shown, do not take this stitch too close to the above stitching (fig. 4).

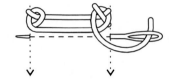

fig. 4.

Step 5 Lift up and slide the needle under the chain on the left hand side (fig. 5) Pull firmly here.

Step 6 Loop thread across to the right hand side and lift up and slide needle under the chain on the right hand side (fig. 6). Now repeat step 4, taking the needle across from the right to the left through the fabric. Steps 4,5 and 6 * -* are repeated to continue this stitch.

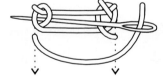

fig. 5.

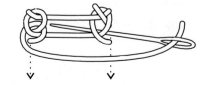

fig. 6.

TURKEY STITCH

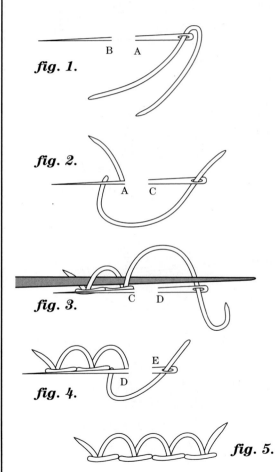

fig. 1.

fig. 2.

fig. 3.

fig. 4.

fig. 5.

Take a small stitch from A-B leaving about 2.5cm (1") of thread trailing as shown fig 1.

With thread below the needle but in line with the A and B go down at C and come up at A. Pull this stitch firmly, holding on to the loose end of thread so that it does not pull right through the material fig. 2.

With the thread above the needle, go down at D, come up at C. This time leave a loop as shown. I find it easier to make all the loops the same length if I insert a knitting needle through the loop and then pull the thread firmly round the needle fig. 3.

With the thread once more below the needle go in at E and come out at D, pull the thread tight fig. 4.

Continue along the line coming up each time into the hole made by the previous stitch. The thread is alternately above the needle (around the knitting needle) creating a loop, and below the needle when it is drawn tight. The finished effect is of a single line of stitching fig. 5.

Work this stitch in lines one above the other holding the stitches already worked down out of the way with your thumb. The closer together the stitches are worked and the closer together the rows are worked the thicker the loops will be and the more luxuriant the end result. Once the shape is filled cut all the loops to the desired length about 3mm (1/8"). Do not cut the rows individually.

DETACHED BUTTONHOLE

Detached buttonhole produces an attractive, solidly stitched shape when worked in a firm twisted thread such as Perle 8 or Coton a broder 16. The stitches are detached from the fabric but held securely in place by the chain foundation. It is important when working detached buttonhole stitch that the stitching is parallel with the base. If it is not worked as shown it makes working 'lifted up' detached buttonhole at a later stage more difficult. To make stitching simpler to execute use a blunt ended tapestry needle to avoid picking up the ground fabric.

To work detached buttonhole stitch the entire shape to be filled must be outlined with small neat chain stitches using a No. 8 embroidery or crewel needle.

Detached buttonhole stitch is worked in one direction - from left to right. The thread is returned from right to left with a long straight stitch.

To start, using a No. 24 tapestry needle, bring the thread to the front at the top left hand corner as shown, from this point the needle does not enter the material again until finishing. Work detached buttonhole stitch across the row of chains only working into the lower loop of the chain stitch (fig. 1).

At the right hand side the needle is taken under and up into the inner loop of the chain stitch then the thread is taken back across the work to the left hand side where it goes under then up into the inner chain stitch loop of the left hand side of the shape. Now continue working detached buttonhole stitch into each loop of the stitch above and catching the straight thread underneath as well (fig. 2). Do not catch the fabric.

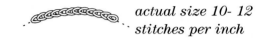

actual size 10- 12 stitches per inch

fig. 1.

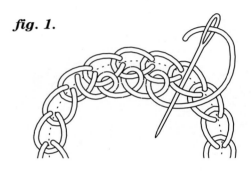

fig. 2.

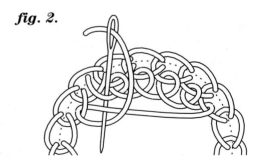

Lifted up Detached Buttonhole

fig. 1.

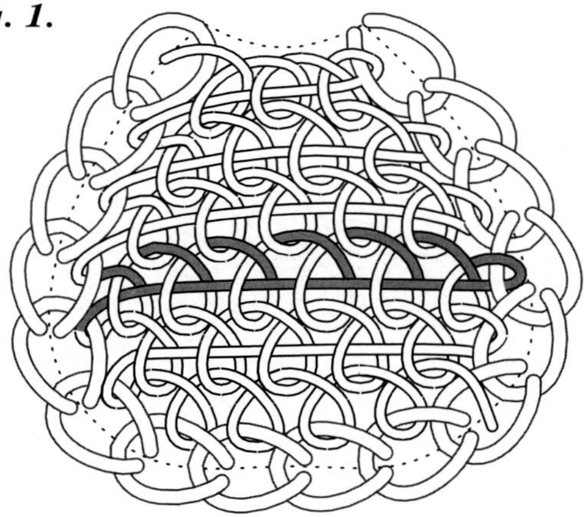

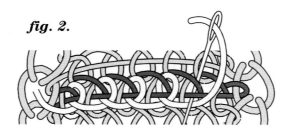

The shaded threads are the threads to work the first row of buttonhole stitch across

The three dimensional effect created using this technique gives great charm and instant eye appeal to your embroidery.

First the area must be completely covered with detached buttonhole stitch which has been padded a little in the usual way. The padding raises the stitching a little making the lines of stitching easier to see.

With the base completed, thread a sharp pointed needle (crewel No 8) with thread and start to work lifted up detached buttonhole stitch by working buttonhole stitch across the required width (marked on designs). The shaded area on figure 1 illustrates the threads this first row of buttonhole stitch will be worked across. Figure 2 shows the first row of buttonhole stitch being worked. Sometimes it is easier to stitch your base line by turning your work upside down as this petal has been and as I did with the bird and one of the mouse's ears. Work from left to right. Loop the thread back to the left hand side ready to continue stitching and change to a tapestry needle. Bring your needle under then up into the loop of the first buttonhole stitch you worked on the left hand side.

fig. 2.

*To improve clarity the figures from this point on **do not** show the stitching beneath them.*

fig. 3.

Leave the thread a little loose, but keep it out of the way until you have inserted your needle into the loop of your first buttonhole stitch. To achieve the desired shape for your lifted up detached buttonhole stitching you may find it useful to place a pin on both sides of the loop (fig 3). With the pins in place tighten your thread and continue working lifted up detached buttonhole stitch across the row in the loops formed in the row above taking your needle down under the straight thread you brought across. As the work is executed in the air it can be useful to hold your thumb under the stitches you are working to keep them separate from the underneath stitching.

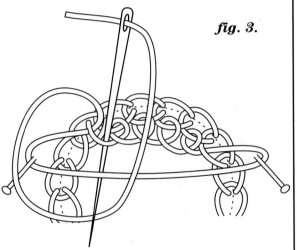

You may find it helpful if you hold the thread to the desired shape with pins while you stitch as stitched for mouse ear B page 67

TO INCREASE IN LIFTED UP DETACHED BUTTONHOLE STITCH
At times when you are using this stitch you will need to increase or decrease to create the desired shape. To increase, at the beginning of a new row work two buttonhole stitches into the first loop and again into the last loop at the end of the row. Sometimes it is necessary to increase in the centre also. To do this two stitches are worked into one loop at the centre fig. 4.

fig. 4.

An extra buttonhole stitch is worked at the beginning and end of the row, and if necessary an extra stitch could be worked in the centre also.

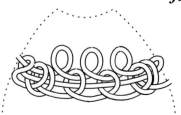

to decrease

fig. 4.

TO DECREASE IN LIFTED UP DETACHED BUTTONHOLE STITCH

Finish the row, loop the thread across to the left into the first stitch as before, but do not put the needle back into this same loop - work the first stitch this row into the next loop. Work across to the end, do not work into the last stitch at the end of the row, work your last stitch into the second to last loop fig 4.

If you wish to create a lifted up point, continue decreasing in this way until a point has been created.

TO FINISH

To neaten the working thread when you have completed your lifted up buttonhole shape just whip down the side until the base of the lifted up stitching is reached. Take the thread to the back of the work and anchor with a couple of little back stitches.

TO FINISH OR CHANGE THREAD COLOUR
WHEN STITCHED IN LIFTED UP DETACHED BUTTONHOLE STITCH.

To finish an old thread or change to a different colour in the middle of the lifted up stitching, whip the old thread down the side and then take it through to the back and anchor. Bring in the new colour or thread on the right hand edge of the lifted up section, work a little back stitch on the lifted up embroidery and then loop the new thread across in the usual manner and continue working detached buttonhole stitch with the new thread. The start of the new thread is covered with buttonhole stitch so that the threads are firmly secured and your starting point hidden.

HANDY HINT

Always start a new lifted up petal with a new thread

OTHER STITCHES THAT CAN BE USED

STRAIGHT STITCH

BACK STITCH

FLY STITCH

FEATHER STITCH

SATIN STITCH

STEM STITCH

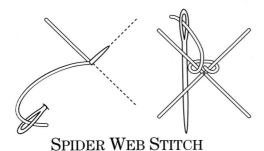

SPIDER WEB STITCH

LONG AND SHORT STITCH

FRENCH KNOT STITCH

GENERAL STITCHING NOTES

HOW TO STITCH LETTERS AND SHAPES.

Detailed stitching instructions are given for each of the designs which appear in this book. I have included methods I have found helpful when stitching this technique, don't hesitate to experiment or try things another way! What suits one person will not necessarily suit the next as this is a creative technique and as such is constantly evolving.

TO STITCH THE LETTERS OF THE ALPHABET

Throughout this book the letters have been stitched using ladder stitch which is a rich textured stitch used extensively in Elizabethan embroidery. However it may be replaced with one row of chain stitch, two rows of chain stitch worked side by side, one row of whipped chain stitch or one row of chain stitch and one row of stem stitch worked side by side with one side of the chain stitch and the stem stitch whipped together. All these alternatives create a very textured effect and would look most attractive. Choose the alternative you enjoy working with.

I recommend stitching using Perle 8 or Coton a broder 16 with the colour of your choice threaded in a Crewel No 8 needle. For my grandchildren I used DMC 367 Coton a broder 16, other colours were used for the other letters and these are given with the instructions for each design.

Each letter has numbers and arrows showing where to start stitching, and the direction in which to stitch. I now tend to stitch each letter the way I write the letter as it seems to be easier to get nice curves this way but I didn't always do this so stitch the way you find it easiest, it is a personal choice.

When you stitch a letter with a break in the stitching, finish the thread on one side of the break and re-start after the break, carrying threads in this type of stitching could well cause a pucker.

TO STITCH THE FLOWERS AND FAUNA

Detailed stitching advice is given with each design. Some general advice is given here.

STITCHING A CURVED SHAPE

When you have a shape with an indented outer edge at the top extra stitching is required in each of the curved sections. Start the filling stitch at the outer left edge of the curve on the left hand side. Stop when you have filled in that section. Move to the outer left edge of the curve on the right hand side and with the same needle and thread work until you have completed that section, still using the same needle and thread now work across the whole area always keeping the stitching parallel to the base (fig 1). Sometimes it can be helpful to draw lines onto your fabric (use a pencil, water erasable pen or fine tip spirit marker) as a guide and remember beads can be used most successfully to cover the odd 'glitch'. To work *down* into curved areas work the right hand area first then the left so that the thread is in the correct position to loop across and continue stitching in second area (fig 2).

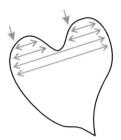

fig. 1.

Stitching a curved shape

STITCHING INTO POINTS

There are many quite tight points which need to be stitched neatly, keeping the points sharp, to look attractive, for example leaves, squirrel ears etc.

When the points are at the top of your stitching start the filling stitch at the tip of the point on the left hand side. Stop at the bottom of the 'V' (fig 3). Move to the tip in the centre with the same needle and thread and work down to the bottom of that shape, stop. Repeat in the same manner with the third tip then work with the same needle and thread across the whole area. You may prefer to stitch all your shapes so that you start with the pointed areas. Alternatively I find in some instances I prefer to work *down* into points. Stitch the right hand point first then take the thread to the next area to the left. Your thread is in the right position to loop across and continue detached buttonhole stitch.

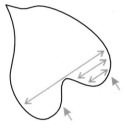

fig. 2.

Stitching down into a curved shape
Bring thread back up at 'x' ready to
continue stitching

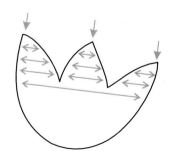

fig. 3.

Stitching into Points

PADDING

Elizabethan embroidery is very textural. This texture is created not only by the stitching but also with a little padding. When you are one row away from completing the stitching of the area you are filling, stop stitching. Take a small piece of very soft dacron padding, and using blunt-nosed scissors push it high up inside the shape - do not make it into a hard lump. Make sure there are no wisps of dacron sticking down into the area yet to be stitched and work the final row of filling stitch.

TO FINISH STITCHING

To close curved designs such as petals or blossoms finish through the centre of the chain stitch which is around the shape outline, take the thread to the back of the embroidery and work two or three back stitches to anchor the thread, clip.

If a sharp point is required as in leaves or the daisy flower, slip stitch the detached buttonhole work down through the fabric on the inner side of the chain stitch point but not actually going through it. Take thread to the back of the work and secure with two or three back stitches, clip.

CHANGING COLOURS

Elizabethan needlewomen frequently changed colours when they were stitching the filling stitches and it is very easy to do. When working detached buttonhole, finish the row, take your thread to the back and neaten off. Bring your new thread to the front on the right hand side loop across to the left and carry on stitching normally. The use of modern random dyed threads will give the same effect.

FINISHING THREADS

Take your thread through to the back and neaten off with a little back stitch or two.

*"In some form or other
the letters we recognise as the alphabet
have been in continuous use for more than
three thousand years"*[5]

The Alphabetic Labyrinth, Johanna Drucker

All chain and ladder stitch to be worked using crewel No. 8 needle.

All picot and detached buttonhole to be worked using a tapestry No. 22-26 needle.

Arrows indicate where to start stitching and the direction in which to stitch rows.

LETTER

The letter A is worked in ladder stitch with thread the colour of your choice. 'A' is worked in three separate movements. The starting position of each stroke is numbered in order of working. Start at the lower left hand tip and stitch following arrows. The cross bar is worked over the top of the previously worked second stroke. The area shown by dotted lines is not stitched. This space is where the forget-me-nots are placed. If you plan to include a different shape allow for this when stitching A.

When you stitch a letter with a break in the stitching, finish the thread and re-start after the break, carrying threads could cause puckers. Refer to colour photograph of Sara page 49.

STRAWBERRIES see Sara page 49

These strawberries look good enough to eat, a reminder of summer treats! They are a useful design, suitable for trailing around any letter or used individually are an attractive decoration for cards and jar covers.

Fruit - Outline all the strawberries in chain stitch using variegated red thread (DMC Perle 8). Still using the same thread fill with detached buttonhole starting at the tip. Pad a little and close. If plain red thread is used sew red seed beads over the worked strawberries for embellishment.

Sepals – Using three threads of sepal green stranded cotton work sepals in picot stitch.

Stem – this is worked in chain stitch using three threads of sepal green stranded cotton.

THREADS

DMC Perle No. 8 - Variegated red 57/Coton a broder 16 - 349 orange/red

DMC stranded cotton
3345   Sepal green
799   blue (forget-me-not flower)
white   strawberry blossom

start stitching here ⟶
direction of rows ⟷

BLUE FORGET-ME-NOT FLOWER OR STRAWBERRY FLOWER
see Baby page 53

This dainty little flower is useful in baby designs where its small size seems entirely appropriate or on a larger design where it is useful for filling the odd space.

Such a small and dainty outline needs a fine thread, outline the petals in chain stitch using one thread of blue stranded cotton, work a few small running stitches as padding and still using the same thread fill with detached buttonhole starting at the tip of the petal and working in to the centre. To make this into a strawberry flower work the petals in the same way but use white stranded cotton. Finish the centre with a French knot in yellow for the forget-me-not and a small white or pale yellow bead for the strawberry blossom.

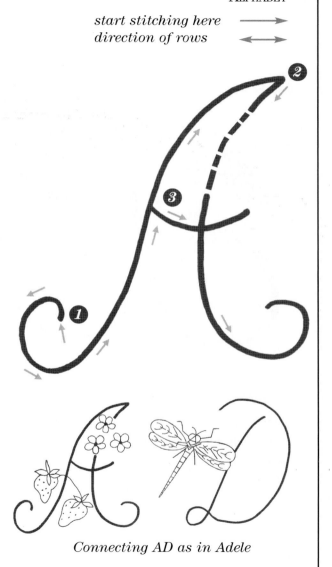

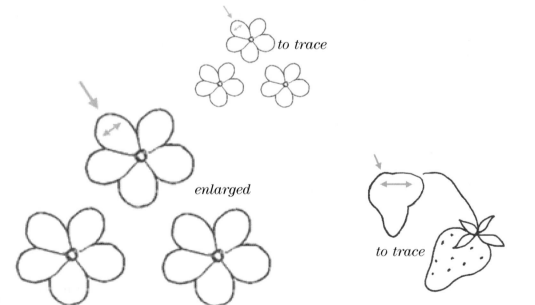

to trace

enlarged

to trace

Connecting AD as in Adele

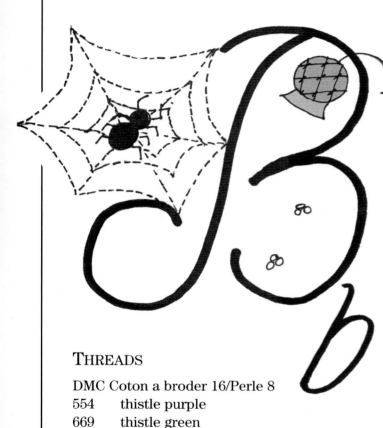

THREADS

DMC Coton a broder 16/Perle 8
554   thistle purple
669   thistle green
Black stranded cotton
Silver and gold metallic thread

All chain, turkey, back and ladder stitch to be worked using a crewel No. 8 needle.

All detached buttonhole to be worked using a tapestry No. 22-26 needle.

Arrows indicate where to start stitching and the direction in which to stitch rows.

LETTER

The letter B is worked in ladder stitch with thread the colour of your choice. 'B' is worked in three separate movements. The starting position of each stroke is numbered in order of working. Start at the top of the vertical stroke and stitch following arrows. Embellish lower section of B with beads.

Refer to colour photograph on pages 54 - 55 as in Blake and Bradley.

SPIDER WEB **see Grandchildren's Gallery pages 54 - 55**

A spider's web is a thing of beauty. Growing up in Central Otago (New Zealand) and experiencing hoar frosts in winter, the ethereal beauty of a frosted spider's web on a fence or bush is unforgettable. Do create these webs around and through your letters, children just love them.

Do not draw this on your fabric (the lines may not be hidden by your stitching) but embroider freestyle in back stitch with silver metallic thread. Start from an outer point, completing each circle before moving into the next, stitch the straight lines last.

(If you really feel you need a guide for stitching the spider's web work one with running stitches and pull it out as you go.)

SPIDER **see Grandchildren's Gallery pages 54 - 55**

The spider is created with two black beads, a small one (4mm 3/16") for the head and a bigger one (8mm 3/8") for the body. Position where required and sew in place. Back stitch legs and feelers (8) using a single thread of black stranded cotton.

SCOTCH THISTLE **see Grandchildren's Gallery pages 54 - 55**

Thistles grow thoughout the world and while a pest for the agriculturalist they are an attractive subject for needlewomen.

Calyx - Outline calyx in chain stitch with thistle green. Still using the same thread fill the area with detached buttonhole starting near the stem. Pad a little and close. Embellish with gold metallic thread, lay three gold threads across the calyx each way and hold in position with a small stitch where the threads cross, see diagram.

Flower - Embroider flower by working four rows of turkey stitch in thistle purple. Turn the thistle upside down and work turkey stitch from the calyx out, holding the competed stitches down as you work. Clip and 'fluff' up. For more information on Turkey stitch see page 18.

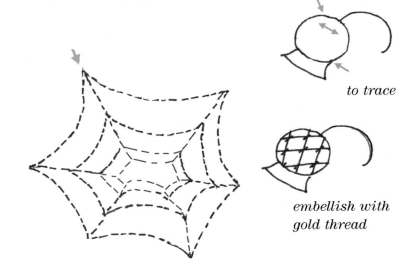

to trace

embellish with gold thread

Connecting BL as in Blake

All, ladder, stem, straight, satin, back stitches and French knots to be worked using a crewel No. 8 needle. Picot stitch is easier worked with a tapestry needle, No. 22-26

Arrows indicate where to start stitching and the direction in which to stitch rows.

LETTER

The letter C is worked in ladder stitch with thread the colour of your choice. It is worked in one movement starting at the top, follow arrows.

LAMB see Anne page 51

Mary's lamb may have had a fleece as white as snow but those near us do not! There is nothing quite so special as a handmade gift for a baby and a blanket with dancing lambs would be treasured.

Ears - these are worked in satin stitch using medium ecru. Start at the tip and stitch across each ear working back to to the head, repeat for the second ear.

Head, neck and top of the legs - these areas are worked in French knots (three wraps around the needle) using black.

Body - work in French knots using medium ecru.

Bottom of legs - these are worked in satin stitch using medium ecru with each stitch worked across the leg.

Tail stitched last and worked in picot stitch using medium ecru.

THREADS

DMC Coton a broder 16/Perle 8

469	olive green
840	medium brown
3033	Medium ecru
Black	
Silver metallic thread	

Fence

The gate is worked in satin stitch in medium brown, still using the same thread work the posts in stem stitch. The wires are also worked in stem stitch but using silver metallic thread.

Grass

The grass is worked in straight stitches using olive green, place the stitches where indicated.

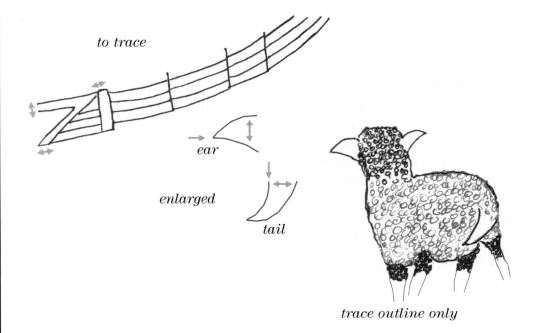

to trace

ear

enlarged

tail

trace outline only

Connect CO with a few stems of grass

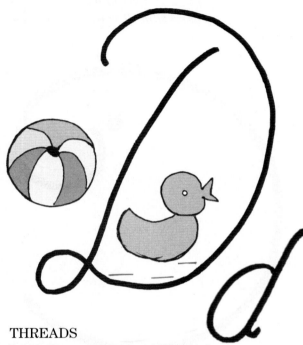

All chain, ladder, satin, turkey and straight stitches to be worked using a crewel No. 8 needle.

All detached buttonhole to be worked using a tapestry No. 22 - 26 needle.

Arrows indicate where to start stitching and the direction in which to stitch rows.

LETTER

The letter D is worked in ladder stitch with thread the colour of your choice. It is worked in one movement, start where indicated and work following the arrows.

Where the line crosses an area already worked I usually stitch over the top of the existing line, but this is optional. Refer colour photograph Bradley page 54.

DUCK **See Emma page 53**

This golden duck brings back happy memories of the shared joy of mother, baby, a warm bath and a bobbing duck - always just out of reach!

Ouline head and body in chain stitch using yellow. Still using the same thread fill the area with turkey stitch working from bottom to top and keeping your thumb on the stitches completed to keep them out of the way. Clip to a length of about 3 mm (1/8"). Finish with a small black bead for the eye and a small blue ribbon bow.

The beak is stitched using orange and working four straight stitches.

THREADS

DMC Coton a broder 16/Perle 8

367	medium green
930	slate blue
932	light bluebell
3326	pink
743	yellow*
818	soft pink
3032	taupe
740	orange*

small black bead and blue ribbon*

* duck requisites

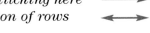

BALL see Emma page 53

No box of toys would be complete without a ball!
Outline the entire ball and sections with chain stitch using medium green then
work satin stitch in the centre still using the same thread. Fill each section with
detached buttonhole starting at the top and working down in slate blue, pink,
yellow, light bluebell, soft pink and taupe.

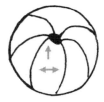

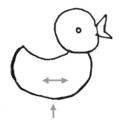

to trace

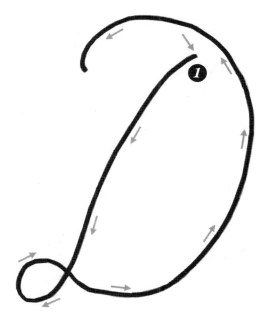

HANDY HINT

Stranded cotton works well for turkey
stitch also as it 'fluffs up' well

Connecting DE as in Debbie

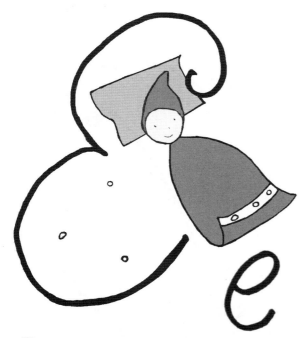

All chain, turkey, ladder stitch and French knots to be worked using a crewel No. 8 needle.

All detached buttonhole to be worked using a tapestry No. 22-26 needle.

Arrows indicate where to start stitching and the direction in which to stitch rows.

Letter

The letter E is worked in ladder stitch using the colour of your choice. It is worked in one movement starting at the top of the letter, follow arrows.

Doll Resting on Pillow **see Emma page 53**

Dolls have been the companions, friends and babies of little girls for generations. This little doll, embroidered on a pillow slip or cot sheet, or as shown here in her name would delight any little girl. It would also look most attractive stitched as part of a nursery scene.

Pillow - Using soft pink outline the pillow in chain stitch and fill with detached buttonhole. Start at the top left hand corner and work across the pillow. Work a complete rectangle for the pillow so that the hood is worked on top of it.

Hood and Face - Outline the hood and face with chain stitch using pink. Fill the hood with detached buttonhole starting at the tip of the hood. Note that this stitching is worked on top of the already stitched pillow. The face is worked in detached buttonhole using pale pink. Highlight the eyes with two French knots worked in blue and the mouth with a straight stitch worked in lip pink. Work one Turkey stitch in dark brown for the hair and clip.

Threads

DMC Coton a broder 16/Perle 8

818   soft pink
3326   pink
3713   pale pink
334   blue
39   lip pink
801   dark brown
three deep pink beads, small blue bow

Bag - Outline in chain stitch with pink, note the little rectangular shape near the base of the bag and outline that in chain stitch also. It is not stitched at all and on completion of the other stitching sew three deep pink beads here as buttons or sew French knots. The main area of the bag is filled with detached buttonhole starting at the left hand side of the neck. Work across the area and pad a little before closing. Highlight with a small bow at the neck.

E can be worked in many different ways, for variations see Grandchildren's Gallery pages 54 - 55. The possibilities are endless, experiment with your favourite shapes to create a design that pleases you!

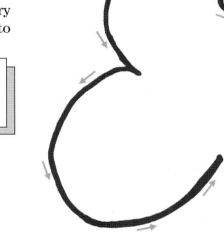

> ## HANDY HINT
>
> Do not embellish baby garments with beads, work French knots instead.

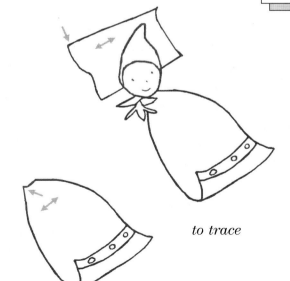

to trace

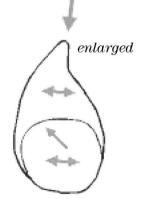

enlarged

Connecting EM as in Emma

All chain, straight and ladder stitch to be worked using crewel No. 8 needle. All detached and lifted up buttonhole stitch to be worked using a tapestry No. 22-26 needle.

Arrows indicate where to start stitching and the direction in which to stitch rows.

LETTER

The letter F is worked in ladder stitch using the thread colour of your choice. It is worked in three separate movements. The starting position of each stroke is numbered in order of working. Starting at the top of the vertical stroke, stitch following arrows. The cross bar is worked over the top of the previous stitching.

BIRD - RIFLEMAN **see Anne page 51**

The Rifleman is New Zealand's smallest bird, stitched here in its nest it will never fly away!

Head and top of body - Chain stitch around the body and through the chest area with grey. Starting where indicated fill the upper body with detached buttonhole in grey working backwards and forwards across the body. Pad a little before you close into the chain stitch across the centre of the chest.

Breast - Working in detached buttonhole throughout, start with ecru and work to the centre of the area, see diagram. Now thread a second needle with citrus yellow and work alternate stitches in ecru and citrus yellow for a couple of rows, complete the area working in citrus yellow only. Pad a little and close.

Tail - The tail is worked in straight stitches using black

Wing - The wing is worked in lifted up detached buttonhole using grey. Turn your embroidery around so that the bird is upside down. Work the first row of stitching into the grey body section where indicated then work a further four to six rows in lifted up detached buttonhole, creating the wing shape shown. Increase and decrease the stitches to create a wing shape see page 20 for detailed information on this stitch.

THREADS

DMC Coton a broder 16/Perle 8

318	grey	436	straw
469	olive green	471	light olive green
727	citrus yellow	801	dark brown
840	medium brown	842	medium straw
3033	medium taupe	Black	

Ecru

gold metallic thread and small black bead

start stitching here ⟶
direction of rows ⟷

Foot, Eye and Beak- Only one foot is showing and this is worked in straight stitches in black. The beak is worked with two little straight stitches also in black, sew one small black bead in the correct position for an eye and your bird is complete.

NEST AND EGGS

Nest - Work the nest with straight stitches using straw, medium straw and dark brown worked in alternating circles one row for each colour.

Eggs - Outline in chain stitch and fill with detached button worked using medium taupe. Pad each egg a little before closing.

BRANCH, TWIGS AND LEAF

Branch and Twigs - Work two rows of chain stitch side by side using medium brown. The twigs are a single row of chain stitch stitched using the same thread.

Leaf - Outline in chain stitch with light olive green and fill with detached buttonhole using olive green, starting at the tip. Pad a little and close. Emphasise the central vein by working it in back stitch with gold metallic thread. The stem is worked in chain stitch using light olive green.

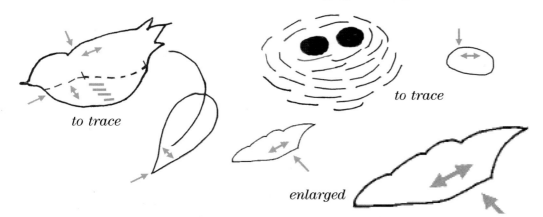

to trace

to trace

enlarged

Connecting FR as in Frances

All chain, stem, straight and ladder stitch to be worked using crewel No. 8 needle.

All detached buttonhole to be worked using a tapestry No. 22-26 needle.

Arrows indicate where to start stitching and the direction in which to stitch rows.

LETTER

The letter G is worked in ladder stitch using thread the colour of your choice. It is worked in one movement starting at the top.

GRAPES

Grapes have been grown for centuries for both winemaking and eating. I live in a grape growing area and the changing leaf colour and maturing fruit tell me autumn has arrived.

Vines - To create the vines work one row of chain stitch in medium brown.

Tendrils - optional work in stem stitch in light olive green

Leaves - Work the spine in stem stitch using two gold metallic threads. To fill the leaf work straight stitches using olive green. Start at the base of the leaf and work from the outer edge of the leaf into the spine. Stem stitch veins using one gold metallic thread.

THREADS

DMC Coton a broder 16/Perle 8

469   olive green

471   light olive green

840   medium brown

Gold metallic thread.

Green or grape coloured beeds

GRAPES

Green or grape coloured beads. Start attaching the beeds at the top left hand side of the bunch and work down finishing with one bead at the tip. Sew on with double invisible thread and shape bunch as you sew.

to trace

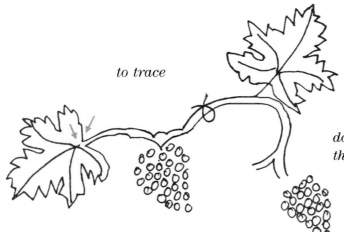

do not trace grapes, indicate the placement of beads only

HANDY HINT

Make a wine carry-bag and sew your initials and the grapes and leaves on it take to your next party.

GA connecting as in Gary

All chain, stem, satin, back and ladder stitch and French knots to be worked using a crewel No. 8 needle.

All detached buttonhole stitch to be worked using a tapestry No. 22-26 needle.

Arrows indicate where to start stitching and the direction in which to stitch rows.

LETTER

The letter H is worked in ladder stitch, in three separate movements with thread the colour of your choice. The starting position of each stroke is numbered in order of working. Start at the top left hand tip and stitch following arrows. The cross bar is worked over the top of the long right hand stroke The dotted lines are not stitched - this space is where I have positioned the lady bird. If you have different shapes to embroider, allow for these. Remember to finish your threads off at one edge of a break in the lettering and start afresh on the other side.

For different treatments of H see Grandchildren's Gallery, pages 54 - 55 Heath and Joshua.

THE CORNFLOWER **see Hope page 55 and Anne page 51**

The Cornflower is a favourite with gardeners and it is a particularly appealing flower, worked with or without lifted up petals it looks most attractive.

FLOWER

Calyx - Outline in chain stitch using olive green, with the same thread fill with detached buttonhole starting at the top on the left hand side. For detailed information on stitching down into points see page 25. Pad a little. To highlight the calyx back stitch around it in gold after the petals have been completed.

Petals - These are stitched in two separate stages.

THREADS

DMC Coton a broder 16/Perle 8
469   olive green
931   medium Bluebell
932   light Bluebell
gold metallic thread

Step 1 - Outline the lower section of each petal (long dashed line) using light bluebell. Still using the same thread and starting at the top left hand point fill the area with detached buttonhole, pad a little and close.

Step 2 - Next chain stitch in medium bluebell from the calyx down to the already worked section of the petal (the dotted line) Still using medium Bluebell fill with detached buttonhole starting at the top work down to the lower section of each petal. Work into the chain stitch across the top of the lower section of the petal and then work the the rest of the petal in lifted up detached buttonhole stitch. See page 20 for detailed instructions on working lifted up detached buttonhole stitch and increasing and decreasing to create the same shape as the lower section of the petal which has already been worked.

The stem is worked in stem stitch using olive green.

The instructions for stitching the ladybird are given on page 87.

The cornflower is shown in EEE and FEC but is stitched differently in each of these books.

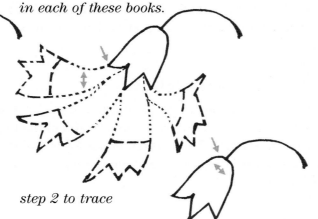

step 1   *step 2 to trace*

The Caterpillar is good for connecting, see HA

All chain, straight and ladder stitch and French knots to be worked using crewel No. 8 needle.
All detached buttonhole to be worked using a tapestry No. 22-26 needle.
Arrows indicate where to start stitching and the direction in which to stitch rows.

LETTER

The letter I is worked in ladder stitch with thread the colour of your choice. It is worked in one movement starting at the top left hand tip.

The following designs are ideal for use in a child's room, on their name like this or they could be stitched to make a nursery scene.

TEDDY **see Emma page 51**

The Teddy is a favourite toy that now comes in all shapes and sizes.
Using taupe thread throughout, outline each section of the teddy bear in chain stitch and fill with detached buttonhole stitch. Each part of the body is worked seperately and padded as it is completed. Refer to the diagram for where to start stitching. Attach two small black beads for eyes and embroider the nose and mouth with one thread of black stranded cotton. Decorate with a small blue bow at the neck.

BLOCKS **see Emma page 51**

A - Outline with straight stitches in bright red. Work 'A' in three straight stitches. The side flower is three French knots worked in the bright red with three small straight stitches worked in medium green for leaves.
B - Worked as for 'A' only using medium green for the outline and 'B' and pink for the flower.

THREADS

DMC Coton a broder 16/Perle 8
3326	pink
930	slate blue
743	yellow
818	soft pink
3032	taupe
321	bright red
367	medium green

black stranded cotton
2 small black beads, blue ribbon

RATTLE see Emma page 51

Using soft pink outline the knob and rattle in chain stitch and work two rows of chain stitch side by side between the two to form a handle. Fill both the knob and rattle with detached buttonhole stitch starting where indicated and pad a little before closing. The rattle is decorated with rows of chain stitch worked over the top of the padded area in pink, slate blue and yellow. The ribbon is worked in ladder stitch using pink.

to trace

Connecting IN

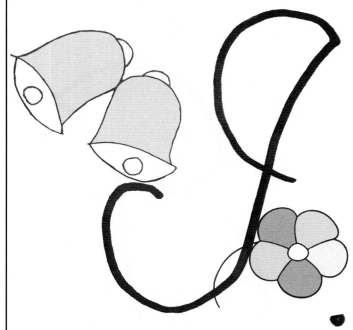

All chain and ladder stitch to be worked using a crewel No. 8 needle.

All detached buttonhole stitch to be worked using a tapestry No. 22-26 needle. Arrows indicate where to start stitching and the direction in which to stitch rows.

LETTER

The letter J is worked in ladder stitch using the thread colour of your choice. 'J' is worked in two separate movements. The starting position of each stroke is numbered in order of working. Start where indicated and stitch following arrows, where the stitching crosses an already worked section stitch on top of the earlier stitching.

WEDDING BELLS **see Wedding Ring Pillow page 52**

Thoughtful details enhance a Wedding Celebration. A beautiful bridal ring pillow exquisitely stitched and handcrafted from the silks, pearls and beading of the gown makes a perfect addition to a very special day. I stitched two bells and and used small pearl beads to outline two hearts see page 52. An arrangement of some of the flowers given in this book would also be most attractive.

Stitch the top of each bell in chain stitch and then chain stitch the outline. Fill the main area with detached buttonhole stitch. Starting at the top of the bell and working down. Note the lower area is not stitched, sew a large (6mm 1/4") pearl bead here to complete.

THREADS

DMC Perle 8/Coton a broder 16
Wedding Bells
Cream
Blossom
224   medium Paris pink
223   dark Paris pink
stranded cotton
3345   sepal green

BLOSSOM AND BUD **see Bradley page 54 and Sara page 49.**

Directions here are for the blossom stitched using medium Paris pink throughout, colours for a 'deep red' blossom are given with 'Sara' on page 90, if used for a Wedding Ring Pillow you may prefer to stitch it in cream.

Flower Centre - chain stitch around the centre.

Petals - Outline each petal in chain stitch. Start stitching at the outer edge of each petal, work towards the centre of the flower and fill each petal with detached buttonhole stitch. Pad each petal a little before closing.

Filiaments - Now work one straight stitch between each petal using three threads of sepal green stranded cotton and sew a small pearl at the end of each stitch. To complete sew a 4mm pearl to the centre.

Bud - Outline the bud in chain stitch using medium Paris pink and starting at the tip fill with detached buttonhole using dark Paris pink. To complete stitch three straight stitches and sew a small white pearl at the end of each straight stitch.

Stems - These are worked in chain stitch in sepal green using three threads of stranded cotton.

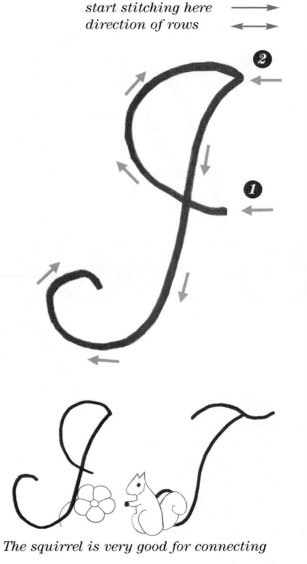

start stitching here
direction of rows

The squirrel is very good for connecting

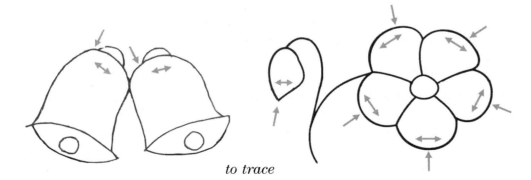

to trace

All chain, fly, back, straight and ladder stitch to be worked using crewel No. 8 needle. All detached buttonhole to be worked using a tapestry No. 22-26 needle. Arrows indicate where to start stitching and the direction in which to stitch rows.

LETTER

The letter K is worked in ladder stitch using thread the colour of your choice. 'K' is worked in three separate movements. The starting position of each stroke is numbered in order of working. Start at the top left hand tip and stitch following arrows.

The dotted lines in K are not stitched. This space is where the lady bird sits. If you have different shapes to embroider remember to allow for these. Do not carry the thread across the break in stitching as it is likely to cause puckers in your finished work, rather stop, finish the thread then restart on the other side of the break.

PEACOCK

One of the showiest of all birds because of its great size and the beauty of its feathers, it has been admired for centuries and is mentioned by Aristophanes in 'The Birds' written in Greece 400BC. The peacock is a very 'luscious' design to include in your embroidery and adds richness and depth. Despite being quite a large design I find it can be used most effectively between letters or at the finish of a word see Grandchildren's Gallery pages 54 - 55.

HEAD AND BODY

Outline the head and body, including the two wing outlines, in chain stitch using peacock blue. Still using the same thread fill with detached buttonhole starting at the top of the head. Note the two wings are stitched separately to give the peacock a nicely curved body. Pad a little and close. The beak is created by stitching three very small fly stitches, worked closely together, in citrus yellow.

THREADS

DMC Coton a broder 16/Perle 8
669   peacock green
796   peacock blue
727   citrus yellow
Black stranded cotton
Gold metallic thread
Blue sequins and black seed beads

BABY'S BIB AND CARDS

51

WEDDING RING PILLOW AND CHINA BOWL LID

BRADLEY

HEATH

GRANDCHILDREN'S GALLERY

BLAKE

HOPE

JOSHUA

GRANDCHILDREN'S GALLERY

TAIL

Outline the tail in chain stitch using peacock green. Starting at the lower edge of the tail fill with detached button hole. Pad a little and close. Peacock's have glorious tails and this one is no exception. Sew blue sequins over the tail using either invisible or matching thread then stitch around each sequin in back stitch using gold metallic thread. To finish the tail I work 'fringe knots' around the base of the tail where indicated. I find these are easier to work through the chain stitch than anything else. Cut peacock green thread into 4cm (1 1/2") lengths, take one length of thread, fold in half and thread the ends through one loop of the chain stitch. Take the ends back through the loop of the folded thread and tighten. Cut and trim to desired length then 'fluff up'.

To finish - work four straight stitches on top of the Peacock's head using one thread of black stranded cotton and sew a black seed bead at the end of each extension to complete. Sew a small black bead in the right position for the eye. To highlight the lower edge of the Peacock's wings work fly stitches in gold thread on each wing.

LADYBIRD see instructions with 'Z' on page 86

fringe knots

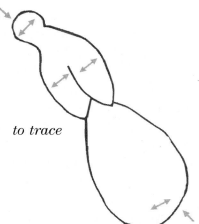

to trace

K joined to E as in Blake

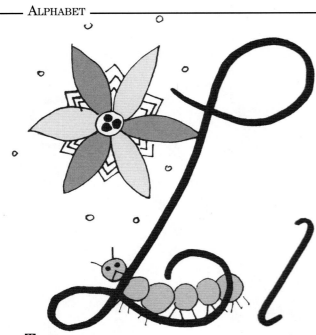

Threads

DMC Coton a broder 16/Perle 8

469   olive green*
471   light olive green*
562   mint green
758   pale apricot
945   dark apricot

black stranded cotton
two black seed beads for caterpillar's eyes
and three apricot drop beads for stamen of
flower, small beads to match flower
*caterpillar

The colours given here are for stitching an 'apricot' flower, colours for a 'red' version are given on page 91.

All chain, fly, back and ladder stitch to be worked using crewel No. 8 needle. All detached buttonhole stitch to be worked using a tapestry No. 22-26 needle. Arrows indicate where to start stitching and the direction in which to stitch rows.

Letter

The letter L is worked in ladder stitch using the thread colour of your choice. 'L' is worked in one movement starting at the top left hand tip, stitch following arrows crossing over already worked parts of the letter. Refer colour photograph page 54, Bradley.

Flower gardens became fashionable in the Elizabethan period. The discovery of new countries with new plants fostered this interest which was reflected in the embroidery of the time. Flowers and insects and tiny animals were embroidered in colours which frequently bore no resemblence to their appearance in nature, nor was scale or size a consideration.

Daisy Flower - see 'Anne' page 51 and Sara page 49.

Petals - Chain stitch around the centre and around each petal using pale apricot. Using dark apricot and starting at the tip of each petal work towards the centre filling with detached buttonhole. Pad a little and close.
Flower centre - this is worked on a hedebo ring stick using pale apricot. Ensure the diameter of the ring you are working on is approximately the same size as the diameter of the flower centre and work about four rows of buttonhole stitch to form a nice 'cup'. Sew this to the centre of the flower and then sew three matching beads in the centre to form the stamens. Alternatively on a similar flower in 'Sara' page 49 rather than working a flower centre I sewed a large pearl at the centre to complete the flower.

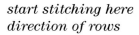
start stitching here
direction of rows

Using mint green thread work three fly stitches between each petal. Surround flower with small pink beads.

CATERPILLAR **see Sara page 49**

Outline the head and each segment of the body in chain stitch using olive green. Each of the segments is filled with detached buttonhole stitch worked using light olive green, refer to the diagram, arrows indicate where to start stitching and direction of rows. Pad each area a little before closing.

Work legs, mouth and feelers in back stitch with one thread of black stranded cotton. Sew two small black beads in position for the eyes.

For a quite different look you could work each section of the caterpillar in a different colour to create a 'jazzy' critter!

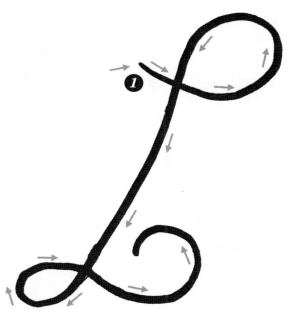

to trace

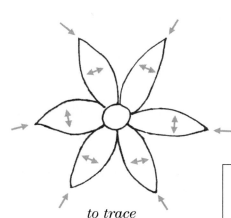
to trace

HANDY HINT

Drop beads have an interesting shape and work well as stamens.

Connecting L and C

THREADS

DMC Coton a broder 16/Perle 8

502   medium sea green
504   light sea green
931   medium Bluebell
932   light Bluebell
black*
gold and silver* metallic thread
silver bugle beads*
* used in the umbrella

All couching, chain and ladder stitch to be worked using crewel No. 8 needle.

All laced chain and detached buttonhole to be worked using a tapestry No. 22-26 needle.

Arrows indicate where to start stitching and the direction in which to stitch rows.

LETTER

The letter M is worked in ladder stitch using the thread colour of your choice. It is worked in four separate movements. The starting position of each stroke is numbered in order of working. Start at the top left hand tip and work, following arrows.

UMBRELLA see Anne page 51

Umbrellas are always fun to work with! Upside down, downside up, in the wind, in the rain, all the colours in the rainbow!

This is definitely a grey day umbrella! Using black thread throughout, chain stitch around the outer edge of the umbrella and fill the umbrella with detached buttonhole, starting where indicated. Pad a little and close. The spines are couched on top of the already stitched umbrella using silver metallic thread.

HANDLE

Using black thread work two rows of chain stitch side by side starting at the top.

RAIN

Scatter some rain drops by sewing on silver bugle beads where indicated.

start stitching here →
direction of rows ↔

BELL-FLOWER see Anne page 51

Chain stitch around the edge and down the centre of each of the sepals first using light sea green.

Next outline the bell-flower in chain stitch using light bluebell. Using medium bluebell, start at the outer edge of the flower and fill the entire area with detached buttonhole stitch. When you start you may need to work an extra row or two into each point before continuing to stitch the main area of the bluebell - see page 25 for stitching into points. Pad a little and close.

Define the curves in the bell-flower by working three rows of chain stitch from the calyx down to the edge of the petal on top of your embroidery using gold metallic thread. Complete the sepals by working laced chain stitch down the centre line of chain stitch using medium sea green.

Stem – this is worked in chain stitch using medium sea green.

Bell flower

to trace

Connect to A with bell flower and raindrops

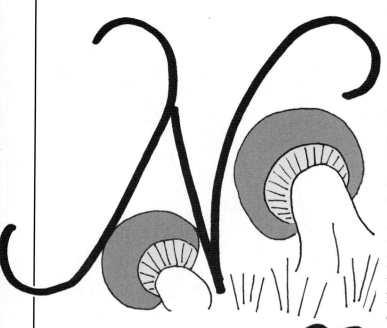

All chain, ladder stitch and straight stitch to be worked using a crewel No. 8 needle.

All detached buttonhole to be worked using a tapestry No. 22-26 needle. Arrows indicate where to start stitching and the direction in which to stitch rows.

LETTER

The letter N is worked in ladder stitch using the thread colour of your choice. 'N' is worked in three separate movements. The starting position of each stroke is numbered in order of working. Start at the top left tip and work, following arrows.

MUSHROOMS **see Anne page 51**

If you take an early morning walk in the fields in autumn you may be rewarded with the sight of mushrooms growing in the grass. They are plants, but not having green leaves or flowers, belong to the fungi family. Chain stitch all outlines including the stalk, spore area and surface of mushroom using medium taupe.

Fill the surface area of the mushroom with detached buttonhole stitch using medium taupe. Refer to the diagram for where to start stitching. Pad the surface area a little and close. For more information on stitching down into curves see page 25.

Continue stitching the spore area with detached buttonhole using taupe refer to the diagram for where to start stitching. Do not pad this area but highlight with straight stitches worked in black over the top of the stitching see diagram. The stalk area is outlined only.

THREADS

DMC Coton a broder 16/Perle 8
469 olive green
3032 taupe
3033 medium taupe
Black

GRASS

Scatter some stalks of grass around the base of the mushrooms by working straight stitches where indicated using olive green.

I have drawn N with two mushrooms but if it appeared in the middle of a name I would probably only use one. A mushroom can be used as a linking design, see O and N linked with a mushroom as in Sharon.

HANDY HINT

Trellis stitch could be used to stitch the Mushroom

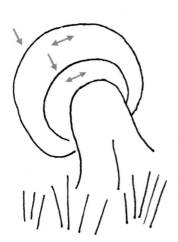

to trace

Joining N with O

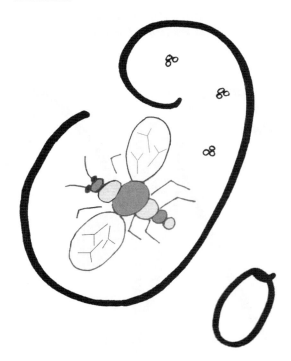

THREADS

DMC Stranded Cotton
White
Black
414   grey
725   daffodil yellow
silver metallic thread

All chain, straight, turkey and ladder stitch to be worked using a crewel No. 8 needle.

All detached buttonhole stitch to be worked using a tapestry No. 22-26 needle. Arrows indicate where to start stitching and the direction in which to stitch rows.

LETTER

The letter O is worked in ladder stitch the thread colour of your choice. It is worked in one movement starting at the left hand tip, stitch following arrows. See Grandchildren's Gallery pages 54 - 55.

BEE see Anne page 51

Bees delight the eye, pollinate the flowers for the gardeners and in embroidery their fluffy body and diaphonous wings add interest wherever they are stitched.

Wing - Outline the wings in chain stitch using two threads of black stranded cotton. Fill the wing area with fly stitches working using one strand of silver metallic thread, starting at the tip.

Head - Using two threads of grey stranded cotton work satin stitch to cover the area.

Body - The body is worked in turkey stitch in alternating rows of yellow and black, finishing with white to create a deliciously fluffy bumble bee! Three threads of stranded cotton are used throughout. Start at the top of the body and work three rows of daffodil yellow then four rows of black, four rows of daffodil yellow, then four more rows of black, finishing with two rows in white. Remember to hold your embroidery so that you are working up the body with completed stitching held under your thumb out of the way!

Legs and Feelers - Using one thread of black stranded cotton work the legs and feelers in straight stitch, refer to diagram for their placement.

Attach two small white beads for eyes.

Instructions for spider's web are given on page 30.

Instructions for spider's web are given on page 30.

start stitching here
direction of rows

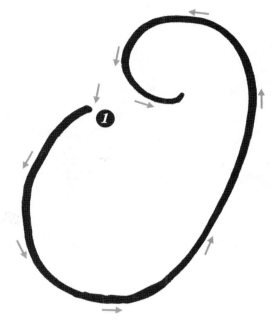

Wing, enlarged detail

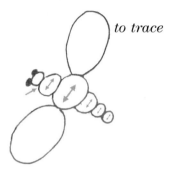

to trace

head
yellow
black
yellow
black
white

enlarged

O connected to P by spider's web

All chain, straight and ladder stitch to be worked using a crewel No. 8 needle. All detached and lifted up detached buttonhole stitch to be worked using a tapestry No. 22-26 needle.

Arrows indicate where to start stitching and the direction in which to stitch rows.

LETTER

The letter P is worked in ladder stitch using the thread colour of your choice. 'P' is worked in two separate movements. The starting position of each stroke is numbered in order of working. Start at the top of the vertical stroke and stitch following arrows.

MOUSE

Little animals like the mouse fit well into this embroidery although they are not found in Elizabethan embroidery their size makes them very suitable.

Body - Chain stitch right round the mouse's body, including the legs, using dark grey. Then using mouse grey fill the entire area with detached buttonhole starting at the nose and working down the legs as you go. Pad a little as you move down the body to give shape.

Ears - The two ears are stitched differently.

Ear A - Turn the mouse upside down and stitching into the chain stitch outline work lifted up detached buttonhole stitch using mouse grey across the area shown to make the base of the ear. See diagram. Loop the thread across in the usual way - you may find it helpful to use a pin to keep the thread firm. Continue working lifted up detached buttonhole stitch decreasing as required to create the desired shape. Finish off by running thread under the back of the ear to the body then take thread to the back and work one or two little back stitches to secure thread. For more information on increasing and decreasing in lifted up detached buttonhole stitch see page 20.

THREADS

DMC Coton a broder 16/ Perle 8
318   mouse grey
413   dark grey
744   hard yellow
black stranded cotton
small wine bead

Ear B - Using mouse grey throughout, work two buttonhole stitches side by side on the body in the appropriate place, these two stitches anchor the ear to the body. From this point on work in lifted up detached buttonhole stitch. To create a nicely rounded ear put a pin each side of the loop to hold it in shape then work. Do this all the way down the ear increasing and decreasing where necessary to create a nicely shaped ear and you will be delighted with the end result. You may find it helpful to practice the ears on a scrap of fabric. Finish off by running the thread underneath the back of the ear into the body.

Tail - this is worked in chain stitch using mouse grey.

Whiskers - stitch three straight stitches each side of the mouse's face stitched using one thread of black stranded cotton or for more authentic whiskers some hairs out of a broom would be a good idea!

Eye - attach a small wine bead in the correct position for an eye.

CHEESE

The cheese is stitched around the outline only in chain stitch using hard yellow

Dotted line where cheese rests against letter 'P'

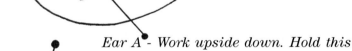

A

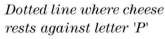

to trace

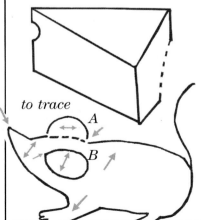

Ear A - Work upside down. Hold this loop with a pin to get a good ear shape

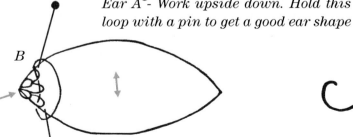

B

Ear B - hold thread to shape with pins

Connecting PH

THREADS

DMC Coton a broder 16/Perle 8
801   dark brown
815   ruby red
904   apple green
gold metallic thread

All chain, ladder stitch and satin stitch to be worked using crewel No. 8 needle. All detached buttonhole and laced chain to be worked using a tapestry No. 22-26 needle.

Arrows indicate where to start stitching and the direction in which to stitch rows.

LETTER

The letter Q is worked in ladder stitch using the thread colour of your choice. It is worked in one movement, starting at the top, stitch following arrows. Where the stitching crosses a previously stitched section of the letter, continue over the top of the earlier stitching. The dotted lines are not stitched. This space is where the cherries sit. If you have different shapes to embroider remember to allow for these. Do not carry the thread across the break in stitching as it is likely to cause puckers in your finished work, rather stop, finish the thread then restart on the other side of the break.

CHERRIES

Cherries in New Zealand signal that Christmas is near! With their beautiful blossoms in spring, fruit in summer and colour in autumn cherry trees are a delight most of the year. These cherries are stitched as a reminder of summer treats!

Cherries - Using ruby red throughout, outline the cherries in chain stitch and fill with detached buttonhole. Start stitching by the stem and work across the cherries. Pad a little and close.

Stalks - The stalks out to each cherry are worked in chain stitch using apple green.

Branch - this is worked in satin stitch using dark brown, work across the branch in short stitches to achieve a more 'realistic' branch.

LEAVES

Using apple green throughout chain stitch around the edge of each leaf and fill with detached buttonhole starting at the tip. Mark the veins with straight stitches using gold metallic thread.

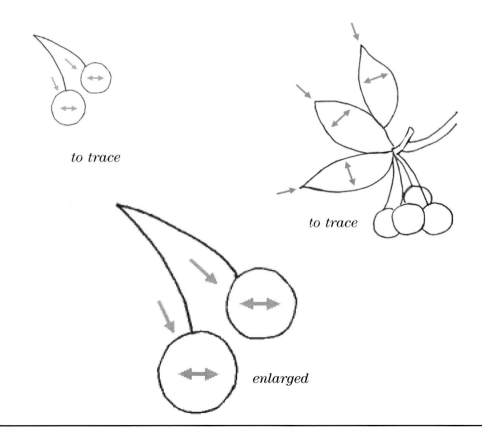

to trace

to trace

enlarged

QU as in Quinn

THREADS

DMC Coton a broder 16/Perle 8
469   olive green
801   dark brown
DMC stranded cotton
3013   light moss green
Gold metallic thread

All running, fly, ladder, stem, satin, and turkey stitch to be worked using a crewel No. 8 needle.

Arrows indicate where to start stitching and the direction in which to stitch rows.

LETTER

The letter R is worked in ladder stitch using the thread colour of your choice. It is worked in three separate movements. The starting position of each stroke is numbered in order of working. Start at the top of the vertical stroke and stitch following arrows.

The dotted lines in R are not stitched. This space is where the gooseberries sit. If you wish to embroider different shapes, allow for these. Do not carry the thread across the break in stitching as it is likely to cause puckers in your finished work, rather stop, finish the thread then restart on the other side of the break

GOOSEBERRIES

Gooseberries are another luscious summer fruit, excellent in pies and fun to gather.

These are worked in satin stitch using four threads of light moss green stranded cotton. Pad the area a little with running stitches then work the first satin stitch taking a long stitch from top to bottom at the centre, continue in satin stitch to one side, then return to the centre and work out to the other side. The markings on the gooseberries are created by working three rows of fly stitch down each gooseberry with gold metallic thread. Work two turkey stitches in dark brown at the top of each gooseberry.

LEAF

The spine and stalk are worked in stem stitch using two threads of gold metallic in the needle together and stitched as one. To fill the leaf work straight stitches using olive green and starting at the base of the leaf work from the outer edge of the leaf into the spine. The veins are created with three large fly stitches worked in doubled gold metallic thread.

To complete sew toning beads to the left of R to balance the design.

to trace

Leaves are useful for connecting

THREADS

DMC Coton a broder 16/Perle 8

349   orange/red
469   olive green
801   dark brown
948   pale peach
3713   dark pink terracotta
White stranded cotton
Silver and gold metallic thread
Three red berries

All chain, fly, straight, French knots, turkey and ladder stitch to be worked using a crewel No. 8 needle.

All detached buttonhole stitch to be worked using a tapestry No. 22-26 needle.

Arrows indicate where to start stitching and the direction in which to stitch rows.

LETTER

The letter S is worked in ladder stitch using thread the colour of your choice. It is worked in one movement starting at the top right hand tip, follow the arrows.

Experience the pleasure of an old fashioned Christmas and discover how enjoyable it is to create that special Christmas atmosphere by making your own small gifts, decorations and cards using some of the designs featured here and on page 83.

SANTA/FATHER CHRISTMAS FACE **see 'Noel' page 56**

Face - using pale peach throughout, outline the face in chain stitch and fill with detached buttonhole starting at the top of the forehead. Pad a little and close. The eyes and mouth are shown with chain stitches and the nose by two French knots all stitched with dark pink terracotta. The beard is worked in turkey stitch using three threads of white stranded cotton. Start at the very bottom of his beard and work up doing the main beard first then work up one side of his face then the other. Hold the stitches you have worked down under your thumb as you work.

Hat -Chain stitch using orange/red around the hat and front band. Still using the same thread fill the hat with detached buttonhole starting where indicated finishing into the top of the band. *Do not* fill the band area. Pad a little and close. Using three threads of white stranded cotton work turkey stitch to fill the band area, clip and 'fluff' up. To create the pom pom work turkey stitch using all six threads of stranded cotton.

Chimney - Work straight stitches where indicated in dark brown

CHRISTMAS STOCKING see 'Noel' page 56

For children Christmas really begins with the discovery early on Christmas morning that their stockings have been mysteriously filled!

Using orange/red outline the stocking in chain stitch and fill with detached buttonhole stitch starting at the top of the stocking. Pad a little and close.

Stocking top - fill the area with turkey stitch using three threads of stranded cotton. Remember to work the rows of turkey stitch from the bottom up. Clip when completed. Finish by working about six straight stitches with silver metallic thread across the top of the boot, but beneath the turkey stitched area.

HOLLY LEAVES see 'Noel' page 56

Outline holly leaves in chain stitch using olive green and using the same thread fill each leaf with detached buttonhole. Starting at the tip work across each leaf and out to each point as you come to it, catching your stitches into the chain stitch points to give a sharply defined leaf shape. Pad a little before closing. Using gold metallic thread work three fly stitches down the centre of each leaf to indicate veins or highlight the central vein with a single straight stitch. Sew three red beads for berries between the holly leaves to complete.

See alternative S's in Joshua page 55 and Sara page 49

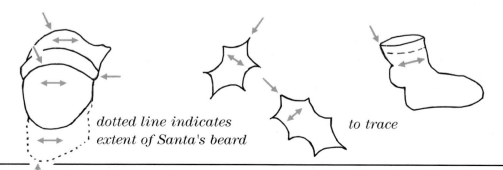

dotted line indicates extent of Santa's beard

to trace

Strawberries are good for connecting

All chain, turkey, fly, stem stitch and ladder stitch to be worked using a crewel No. 8 needle.

All detached buttonhole stitch to be worked using a tapestry No. 22-26 needle. Arrows indicate where to start stitching and the direction in which to stitch rows.

LETTER

The letter T is worked in ladder stitch using the thread colour of your choice. It is worked in two separate movements. The starting position of each stroke is numbered in order of working. Starting at the top of the vertical stroke stitch following arrows. See colour photograph Heath page 54.

SQUIRREL see Grandchildren's Gallery pages 54 - 55

The quick, darting squirrel is much admired for its dexterity and balance, its long fluffy tail makes it an animal that is fun to stitch.

Body - Outline the body, front paw and back legs in chain stitch using medium brown, still using the same thread fill the tip of each ear then the entire body area in detached button hole. Work down the face, out to the nose and into the paw. Close the stitching into the chain stitch outline of the hind leg to highlight the leg when you come down to it, work into the chain from beneath it to continue filling entire area. Pad a little to give a nice rounded shape to your squirrel and close. Next work detached buttonhole in the separate back leg area. See diagram for where to start stitching each section. Pad this area also but less than the body section.

THREADS

DMC Coton a broder 16/Perle 8
471   light olive green
840   medium brown
gold metallic thread
a black bead for the squirrel's eye and a brown bead for the nut

Tail - The tail is worked in turkey stitch. Turn your squirrel around so that you start close to the body and work 'up' the area. Stitch the rows as closely together as you can as the more turkey stitches the bushier the tail! On completion of the stitching, clip and 'fluff up'.

To complete the squirrel attach a small black bead for the eye and sew a small brown bead in position for the nut.

LEAF

Outline the leaf in chain stitch using light olive green and using the same thread fill with detached buttonhole starting at the tip and working across the area as shown. This will ensure that the leaf has nice points. Pad a little and close. Embellish the leaf with veins worked in fly stitch with gold metallic thread. The stem is worked in chain stitch using light olive green.

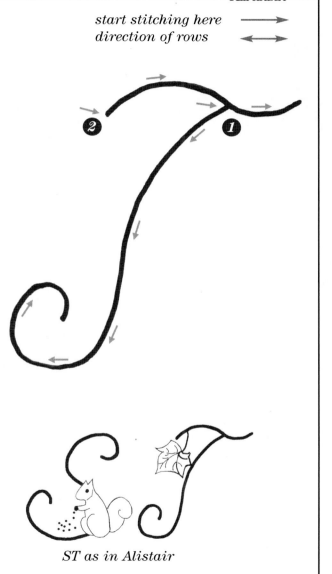

start stitching here
direction of rows

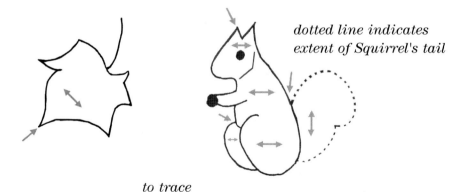

dotted line indicates
extent of Squirrel's tail

to trace

ST as in Alistair

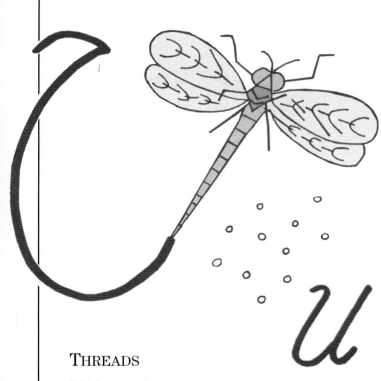

All chain, back, straight, fly, satin and ladder stitch to be worked using a crewel No. 8 needle.

Arrows indicate where to start stitching and the direction in which to stitch rows.

LETTER

The letter U is worked in ladder stitch using the thread colour of your choice. It is worked in one movement starting at the top left hand side. Refer to the colour photograph of Joshua on page 55.

The dotted lines in the U are not stitched. This is where the dragonfly sits. If you prefer you can embroider the U completely or if you have different shapes to embroider, allow for these. If you use a smaller shape and continue stitching beyond the break, do not carry the thread across the break as it is likely to cause puckers in your finished work, rather stop, finish the thread then restart on the other side of the break.

DRAGONFLY see Grandchildren's Gallery pages 54 - 55

Shimmering and shining this larger than life dragonfly will bring a whimsical touch to your embroidery.

Top of Body (shaded area of enlarged detail) – Using two threads of dark sea green stranded cotton work a few small chain stitches for padding then work satin stitch across the shape to cover the area.

Lower Body – Using two threads of slate blue stranded cotton work a few small chain stitches for pading and then work in satin stitch. Work up and down the body starting at the centre, stitch to one side then return to the centre and stitch to the other side. This ensures your stitches are correctly placed and that a nice body shape is achieved. Highlight the lower body with four straight stitches worked where shown using two threads of black stranded cotton.

THREADS

DMC stranded cotton
501   dark sea green
930   slate blue
black
multi-coloured metallic
toning beads

Eyes - These are worked in satin stitch using two threads of black stranded cotton.

Tail - Using all six threads of slate blue stranded cotton take one long straight stitch down the centre of the tail, a shorter stitch on either side will be required to broaden the tail at the top. Couch the tail down at regular intervals using one thread of black stranded cotton.

Wings - Using multi coloured metallic thread throughout, outline the wings in chain stitch, start stitching very close to the body so there are no breaks and fill with fly stitches, starting at the tips.

Legs and feelers - work these in straight stitches using one thread of black stranded cotton.

Sew a sprinkling of toning beads where indicated to add more sparkle to the dragonfly.

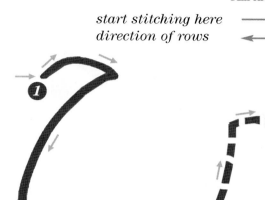

start stitching here
direction of rows

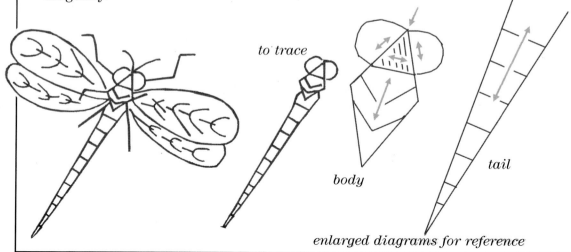

to trace

body

tail

enlarged diagrams for reference

The dragonfly is most useful for connecting to A as in Joshua page 55. Used also mid letters see Grandchildren's Gallery.

All chain, straight, satin, ladder and stem stitch to be worked using a crewel No. 8 needle.

All detached buttonhole stitch to be worked using a tapestry No. 22-26 needle. Arrows indicate where to start stitching and the direction in which to stitch rows.

LETTER

The letter V is worked in ladder stitch using thread the colour of your choice. 'V' is worked in two separate movements. The starting position of each stroke is numbered in order of working. Start at the left hand tip and follow arrows.

FISH see Anne page 51

There are many different shaped and coloured fish that could be stitched. This fish was designed to be part of the decoration round Anne, but you could stitch a multi-coloured or two toned fish and place it on the sea bed, the possibilities are limitless.

Body and tail - Using green throughout, outline the body and tail in chain stitch and fill with detached button hole starting at the mouth. Pad a little and close. Highlight with three fly stitches worked in silver metallic thread.

Fins - Work the fins in satin stitch using green and silver metallic thread in the needle together and stitched as one.

Eye and Mouth - sew a small green bead in position for the eye and make the mouth with one straight stitch using silver metallic thread.

BUBBLES

Sew three or four pearl beads of different sizes in position to indicate bubbles.

WAVES

The waves are worked in stem stitch using royal blue.

THREADS

DMC Coton a broder 16/Perle 8
699   green
796   royal blue
silver metallic thread

start stitching here →
direction of rows ↔

HANDY HINT

The body could be worked using one strand of silver metallic thread in the needle with one thread of green and stitched as one to give a very 'shimmery' fish.

A tropical fish, sea bed plants could be embroidered as bulrushes in 'W'

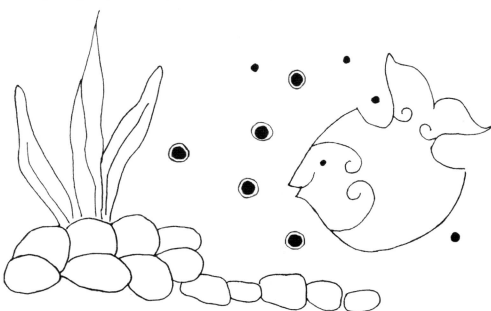

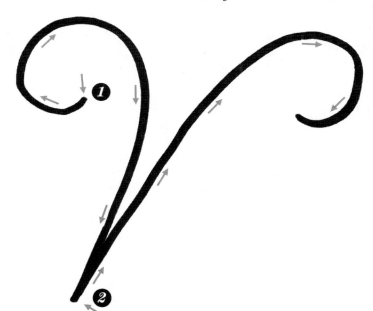

HANDY HINT

All the designs for a name could be on an aquatic theme with crabs, starfish, anchors, life rings, small boats etc!

to trace

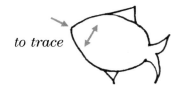

Waves are good for connecting, AV as in David

All chain, French knots and ladder stitch to be worked using a crewel No. 8 needle.

All detached buttonhole to be worked using a tapestry No. 22-26 needle.

Arrows indicate where to start stitching and the direction in which to stitch rows.

LETTER

The letter W is worked in ladder stitch using thread the colour of your choice. 'W' is worked in four separate movements. The starting position of each stroke is numbered in order of working. Start at the left hand tip and follow arrows.

FROG see 'W' page 51

Frogs have a smooth skin which must be kept moist so they always live in or near damp places. I have stitched mine with bulrushes but you could stitch them in the environment where you find them. You could also have fun varying the colours used.

Outline the body and legs in chain stitch with olive green. Starting at the mouth, fill the body area with detached buttonhole using light olive green, padding a little as you go. Close the stitching into the chain stitch outline of the leg to highlight the leg when you come down to it, work into the chain from beneath it to continue filling entire area. The front leg, and feet of both back legs are worked separately see diagram for starting positions.

Sew a black bead in position for the eye or work a French knot in black using two threads of black stranded cotton. Highlight the body with green beads.

BULRUSHS

These are worked in ladder stitch in apple green leaving a space between each stitch to give a 'lighter' look.

THREADS

DMC Coton a broder 16/Perle 8

469   olive green
471   light olive green
842   stone
904   apple green
black stranded cotton or small
black bead
small green beads

STONES

Using 'stone' thread throughout, outline these in chain stitch and fill with detached button hole. Pad a little and close.

to trace

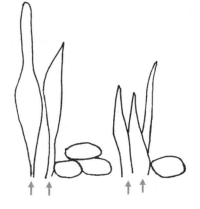

to trace

to trace

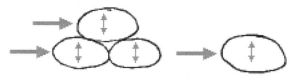

enlarged

Link W to I by continuing bulrushes

THREADS

DMC Coton a broder 16/Perle 8
White
436   caramel
561   dark mint green
798   light royal blue
840   medium brown
3032   taupe
Black stranded cotton
gold metallic and/or silver metallic thread
silver and/or gold beads for decorating the tree

All back, chain, ladder, French knots and satin stitch to be worked using a crewel No. 8 needle.

All detached buttonhole stitch to be worked using a tapestry No. 22-26 needle. Arrows indicate where to start stitching and the direction in which to stitch rows.

LETTER

The letter X is worked in ladder stitch using thread the colour of your choice. 'X' is worked in two separate movements. The starting position of each stroke is numbered in order of working. Starting at the top left hand tip, stitch following arrows. Where the stitching crosses a section of the letter that has already been worked work over the top of the stitching.

CHRISTMAS TREE see 'Noel' page 55

The Christmas Tree is an integral part of Christmas. This tree can be stitched as one element of a design as in 'Noel' or along with all these designs it can be stitched individually for a special Christmas Card or made into Christmas tree decorations.

Tree - Using dark mint green throughout, outline the tree in chain stitch and fill with detached buttonhole starting at the tip of the tree and working down. Stitch across into the tips of the branches catching your stitches into the chain stitch points as you come to them to give good definition to the tree outline. Pad a little as you go and close.

Trunk and tub - work the trunk in satin stitch using taupe, stitching across the trunk. Work the top of the tub in chain stitch using caramel. Decorate the tree with silver or gold beads and stitch a little star at the top of the tree with metallic thread to complete.

PLUM PUDDING see 'Noel' page 55

Plum pudding what could be nicer than hot plum pudding after a delicious Christmas dinner.

Icing - Chain stitch around the top of the pudding in white, starting where indicated fill the area with detached buttonhole, see page 25 for more information on stitching curved areas. Pad a little before closing

Base - Outline the lower area in chain stitch using medium brown and fill with detached button hole starting at the base and working up to the icing. Pad a little and close into the white chain stitch. Work a few black French knots using two threads of black stranded cotton for currants.

Holly Leaves - see instructions with 'S' page 72 but mark the central vein with a straight stitch using gold metallic thread, see picture. Sew three red beads for berries between the holly leaves to complete and you have a Christmas pudding nearly good enough to eat!

BAUBLE see 'Noel' page 55

These simple balls are just some of the decorations which bring about the transformation of the Christmas Tree.
Chain stitch round the ball using light royal blue, still using the same thread fill the area with detached buttonhole. Pad a little and close. Across the middle a line of back stitching has been worked using silver metallic thread (four threads in the needle) to look like zig zag. The top of the bauble is worked in satin stitch using silver metallic thread and the hanging thread is chain stitched using silver metallic thread also.

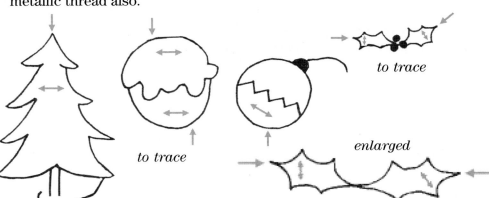

to trace

to trace

enlarged

XM connecting

All ladder stitch and French knots to be worked using a crewel No. 8 needle. Picot stitch is to be worked using a tapestry No. 22-26 needle.

Arrows indicate where to start stitching and the direction in which to stitch rows.

LETTER

The letter Y is worked in ladder stitch using thread the colour of your choice. 'Y' is worked in two separate movements. The starting position of each stroke is numbered in order of working. Start at the top left hand tip and stitch a short stroke. Restart at the right hand tip and stitch the full length stroke. Refer colour photograph Bradley page 54.

RASPBERRIES see Sara page 49

Raspberries bring back childhood memories of glorious colours and juicy taste explosions. These richly textured raspberries are almost good enough to eat. They are worked entirely in French knots (one wrap) using all six threads of stranded cotton. They are stitched in three different groups of colours - the darker shades of red are used to indicate ripe 'ready to eat' berries, slightly lighter shades of red indicate 'almost ripe' berries and shades of green and pale pink are used for those that just need to be left a little longer! Refer to the colour photograph Sara page 49 for the placement of colours.

THREADS

DMC stranded

304	deep red*^
347	dark pink terra-cotta^
754	soft pink+
760	raspberry pink+
815	ruby red*
3013	light moss green+
3328	coral^
3345	sepal green
3772	medium pink terra-cotta^+

Ripe 'ready to eat' berries* are stitched with ruby red and deep red.

*Almost ripe berries^* are stitched with deep red, dark pink terra-cotta, coral and medium pink terra-cotta.

Unripe berries+ combine shades of medium pink terra-cotta, raspberry pink, soft pink and light moss green.

Sepals - work three sepals in picot stitch at the base of each raspberry using sepal green.

start stitching here
direction of rows

to trace

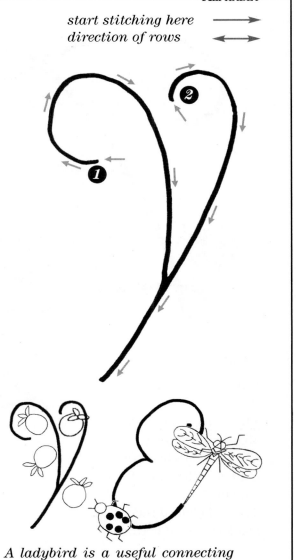

A ladybird is a useful connecting shape

THREADS

DMC Coton a broder 16/Perle 8
Pear
840   medium brown
469   olive green
471   light olive green
gold metallic thread
Ladybird
321   ladybird red
black stranded cotton

All chain, satin, stem, ladder, back stitch and French knots to be worked using crewel a No. 8 needle.
All detached buttonhole stitch to be worked using a tapestry No. 22-26 needle. Arrows indicate where to start stitching and the direction in which to stitch rows.

LETTER

The letter Z is worked in ladder stitch using thread the colour of your choice. It is worked in one movement starting at the top left hand side and following the arrows. Where the stitching crosses a section of the letter that has already been worked stitch over the top.

PEAR see Anne page 51

A fruit second only in popularity to the apple though it is harder to grow.
Fruit - Outline in chain stitch using light olive green. Still using the same thread fill with detached buttonhole starting near the stem and working across the pear. Pad a little and close. Highlight shape marks with gold metallic thread worked in stem stitch.

Leaf - Outline the leaf in chain stitch using olive green, still using the same thread fill with detached buttonhole starting near the tip. Pad a little and close. Highlight the veins by working fly stitch down the centre with gold metallic thread.

Stems - This is worked in satin stitch using medium brown

LADYBIRD see Anne page 51

The bright colours of the ladybird warn predators away but invite the admiration of young and old alike.

Body - The ladybird's body is stitched in satin stitch using ladybird red and finishing each stitch at the centre. Still using the same thread back stitch down the centre.

The head is worked in satin stitch using two threads of black stranded cotton and the spots on the ladybird's back are French knots stitched using three threads of black stranded cotton and five wraps around the needle.

To finish stitch the legs and feelers in back stitch with one thread of black stranded cotton.

ladybird

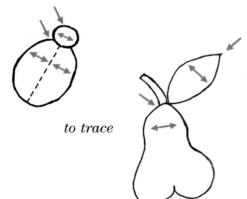

to trace

Connecting PH

match pattern along this line

Refer to the colour photograph of 'Emma' on page 53 for additional detail

The giving of a name is made official on an infant's Birth Certificate but a lovely way for you to mark this special occasion is by embroidering their name accompanied by childhood icons. I selected pink as the basis for the design but changes can be made to the colour of the name or the toys without involving a great deal of extra effort. Changes of this nature would add individuality and charm, you could select colours to echo the colour of the room the embroidery is destined for or colours favoured by the mother. It will quickly become a treasured heirloom and a legacy of love.

REQUIREMENTS
• Choose a firm, closely-woven cream fabric such as crewel linen or similar good quality fabric - 60cm x 30 cm..

• Iron on backing fabric 'stayflex' or similar - 60cm x 30 cm*
• Crewel No 8 and Tapestry 22-26 Needles
• Deep pink beads sewn on background
• Threads, listed below.
*fabric required is given for a name with four capital letters spaced as shown, if your name has more letters you will need more material, alternatively you could stitch an arrangement of Capital and lower case letters, or work the letters closer together. For an alternative design work out your design before purchasing the material.

Trace the design following instructions given on page 9 replacing letters as required and transfer to your fabric. See page 10 for more information on transferring a design and page 9 for more information on creating your own combination of letters and designs. Remember to apply interlining before you start to stitch.

Stitch the letters and motifs following the instructions given in the page numbers below. Your embroidery is not complete without the

match pattern along this line

addition of your name preferably (initials will do) and the date of completion. This embroidery must not be ironed when it is completed, block following the directions given on page 11 and then take your embroidery to your picture framer. Pride in your masterpiece is allowed! You have created an heirloom which may last hundreds of years!

THREADS - DMC Coton a broder 16/Perle 8, unless otherwise stated

EMMA - see stitching instructions with each letter
3328   Coral

DOLL - stitching instructions for this are given on page 36

39	lip pink	334	blue
801	dark brown	818	soft pink
3713	pale pink	3326	pink

three deep pink beads

BLOCKS - stitching instructions for this are given on page 44

321	bright red	367	medium green

BALL - stitching instructions for this are given on page 34

367	medium green	743	yellow
818	soft pink	930	slate blue
932	light bluebell	3032	taupe
3326	pink		

TEDDY - stitching instructions for this are given on page 44

3032	taupe	Black stranded cotton

Two black beads for eyes and small blue ribbon bow

FORGET-ME-NOT - stitching instructions for this are given on page 28
799   blue stranded cotton
Five pearl beads for flower centres

RATTLE - stitching instructions for this are given on page 44

743	yellow	818	soft pink
930	slate blue	3326	pink

DUCK - stitching instructions for this are given on page 34

740	orange stranded cotton	743	yellow stranded cotton

Black seed bead for eye and small blue ribbon bow

match pattern along this line

Refer to the colour photograph of 'Sara' on page 49 for additional detail

Stitched in bright, vivid reds and greens with strong blue lettering this very personal picture cannot help but catch the eye and lift the spirits. It should blend happily with modern or traditional furnishings and become a personal treasure. Vary the colours to your own taste but keep them jewel bright.

REQUIREMENTS

- Choose a firm, closely-woven cream fabric such as crewel linen or similar good quality fabric - 60cm x 30 cm*
- Iron on backing fabric 'stayflex' or similar - 60cm x 30 cm*
- Crewel No 8 and Tapestry 22-26 Needles
- Red and dark blue/green seed beads sewn on background
- Threads, listed below.

*fabric required is given for a name with four capital letters spaced as shown, if your name has more letters you will need more material, alternatively you could stitch an arrangement of Capital and lower case letters, or work the letters closer together. For an alternative design work out your design before purchasing the material.

Trace the design given on page 9 replacing letters as required and transfer to your fabric. See page 10 for more information on transferring a design and page 9 for more information on creating your own combination of letters and designs. Remember to apply interlining before you start to stitch.

Stitch the letters and motifs following the instructions given in page numbers below and on completion of the design motifs, embellish your embroidery by sewing beads to the background. Now sew your initials or name and the date of completion on your embroidery. Do not iron your embroidery when it is completed as this will flatten the

match pattern along this line

texture you have created in your stitching, rather block following the directions given on page 11 and then take your embroidery to your picture framer and look forward to hanging it with pride.

THREADS - DMC Coton a broder 16/Perle 8, unless otherwise stated

SARA - see stitching instructions with each letter
823   dark navy

DRAGONFLY - stitching instructions for this are given on page 76
501   dark sea green   930   slate blue
black stranded cotton   multi coloured metallic thread

BLOSSOM - stitching instructions for this are given on page 46
815   ruby red   469   olive green
five matching deep red beads for the centre of the blossom

STRAWBERRIES   stitching instructions for this are given on page 28
Variegated Red Perle 8, No. 57   3345   sepal green stranded cotton
gold metallic thread

CATERPILLAR - stitching instructions for this are given on page 58
469   olive green   471   light olive green
black stranded cotton   two black seed beads for eyes

DAISY FLOWER - stitching instructions for this are given on page 58
321   bright red   904   apple green
782   mustard   one 4mm (3/16") pearl bead

RASPBERRIES - stitching instructions for this are given on page 84
Ripe raspberries,
304   deep red   815   ruby red
3345   sepal green

Almost ripe raspberries
304   deep red   347   dark pink terra cotta
3328   coral   3772   medium pink terra cotta
3345   sepal green

match pattern along this line

Refer to the colour photograph of 'Noel' on page 56 for additional detail

Decorating for Christmas is a seasonal joy, dressing the tree, putting out special ornaments and rediscovering old favourites acquired or stitched over the years. 'Noel' means joy and peace a wish we all have for the world and our families. The design 'Noel' brings the atmosphere of Christmas into you home and will become a conversation piece with your family and friends. Richly embroidered in reds and greens this design will add to the festive atmosphere in your home.

REQUIREMENTS
- Choose a firm, closely-woven cream fabric such as crewel linen or similar good quality fabric - 60cm x 35 cm*
- Iron on backing fabric 'stayflex' or similar - 60cm x 35 cm*

- Crewel No 8 and Tapestry 22-26 Needles
- Red and dark blue/green seed beads sewn on background
- Threads, listed below

*fabric required is for 'Noel' with four capital letters spaced as shown, if you wish to stitch an alternative greeting that has more letters you will need more material, alternatively you could stitch an arrangement of Capital and lower case letters, or work the letters closer together. For an alternative design work out your design before purchasing the material.

Trace the design given on page 9 and transfer to your fabric. See page 10 for more information on transferring a design and page 9 for more information on creating your own combination of letters and designs. Remember to apply interlining before you start to stitch.

Stitch the letters and motifs following the instructions given in page numbers below. On completion of the design motifs, embellish your

*match pattern
along this line*

embroidery by sewing gold beads to the background. Do sew your initials or name and the date of completion on your embroidery in years to come this will be of great interest to the owner! Do not iron your embroidery when it is completed as this will flatten the texture you have created in your stitching, rather block following the directions given on page 11 and then take your embroidery to your favourite picture framer. Hang this each Christmas and wait for the compliments!

THREADS - DMC Coton a broder 16/Perle 8, unless otherwise stated

NOEL - see stitching instructions with each letter
321 bright red

CHRISTMAS **T**REE - stitching instructions for this are given on page 82
| 436 | caramel | 561 | dark mint green |
| 3032 | taupe | | silver or gold beads to decorate the tree |

BAUBLE - stitching instructions for this are given on page 82
| 798 | light royal blue | | silver metallic thread |

CHRISTMAS **P**UDDING - stitching instructions for this are given on page 82
| 469 | olive green | 840 | medium brown |
| white | | | black stranded cotton |

HOLLY **L**EAVES - stitching instructions for this are given on page 82
| 469 | olive green | | three red beads |

CHRISTMAS **S**TOCKING - stitching instructions for this are given on page 72
| 349 | orange red | | white stranded cotton |
| silver metallic thread | | | |

FATHER **C**HRISTMAS - stitching instructions for this are given on page 72
349	orange red	948	pale peach
3713	dark pink terra cotta	**801**	**dark brown**
white stranded cotton			

STAR
The star is stitching using gold metallic thread, the cross is worked in back stitch with the diagonal threads being long straight stitches couched in place.
Gold beads for background enrichment

Refer to the colour photograph of the 'Ring Pillow' on page 52 for additional detail

Weddings are very special celebrations. Time and thought goes into every aspect of the day especially the clothes to be worn by the bride and her party. A little addition that will look very charming is a Wedding Ring Pillow. It could be made out of the bride's gown and embroidered with flowers used in the bouquet or stitched as this one is with wedding bells, hearts, and the couple's initials interwoven with two rings to symbolise eternity. Cream on cream is perfect to create a truly luxurious pillow.

REQUIREMENTS
- Two pieces of satin or silk 25cm (10") sq.
- Iron on backing fabric 'stayflex' or similar - 25cm (10") sq.
- 1.2 m (1 1/4 yd) of 6 mm (1/4") cream cord or piping
- 60cm (24") of 6mm wide cream ribbon
- 2 x 6mm pearl beads
- packet of size 11 pearl beads
- Cream Perle 8 or Coton a broder 16 and stranded cotton
- Cream machine sewing thread

Transfer the Design
As the fabric used for this design is delicate I transferred the design by tacking it on to the fabric. Trace the outlines of the rings, initials (replacing letters as required) bells and hearts onto a small piece of white tissue paper. Lay the paper over the area to be worked, hold in place with pins or tacking round the edge of the design then tack the design outline using light coloured sewing machine cotton and small stitches. Remove the paper before starting to stitch. Avoid making any more marks than absolutely necessary as you will not be wanting to wash this.

See page 10 for more information on transferring a design and page 9 for more information on creating your own combination of *letters and designs. Remember to apply interlining before you start to stitch.*

Rings - Embroider these with the Perle 8 or Coton a broder 16 in ladder stitch. To ensure your rings are interlocked, start the left hand ring just beneath the top intersection and stitch right round until you are just before the top intersection. Now stitch the right hand ring, working over the top of existing stitching. Finish the left hand ring working over the top of existing stitching.

Initials - embroider these following the instructions given with the letters you use. Stitch in ladder stitch using cream Perle 8 or Coton a broder 16.

Bells - these are worked with the same thread following the instructions given on page 46.

Hearts - Stitch the pearl seed pearls individually to the heart outlines.

Date - add the date in back stitch using two threads of cream stranded cotton

Assembly of the 'Pillow'
Remove all tacking threads. Leave a seam allowance of about 2cm (3/4"), tack piping cord around the edge of the right side of the embroidered design, rounding it at the corners and beginning and ending at the centre bottom.

Place the front and back together with right sides facing and stitch by machine using a zip foot, leave an opening for turning. Clip the piping cord tape at the corners several times. Turn right side out and fill with stuffing. Stitch the opening closed. Cut two 30cm (12") lengths of ribbon and stitch one at either side of the initials ready for the rings.

You are now ready to enjoy the happy day!

match pattern
along this line

match pattern along this line

Refer to the colour photograph of 'Anne' on page 51 for additional detail

In Elizabethan times books were rare and precious. To protect the books beautiful and very richly embroidered covers were made for them and frequently an equally beautifully embroidered cushion was made for the book to be rested upon when in use. 'Anne' was designed as the cover for a book of treasured photographs and memorabilia it would be equally attractive framed.

REQUIREMENTS

- Choose a firm, closely-woven fabric such as crewel linen or similar good quality fabric in the colour of your choice. (For 'Anne' I chose a softer, more loosely-woven linen which was harder to work on.) The quantity required will be determined by the size of the book you wish to cover. Open out the book, measure the front and back and allow for the spine then add 12cms (4 1/2") on each side and 2 cm (3/4") at the top and bottom.
- Iron on backing fabric 'stayflex' or similar, same quantity as for linen
- Crewel No 8 and Tapestry 22-26 Needles
- Threads, listed below

Trace the design replacing letters as required and transfer to your fabric.
Very Important - make sure the design is on the right hand side and centred correctly. It may help if you tack the outer edge of the design so that you can check its placement before transferring the design in detail.
See page 10 for more information on transferring a design and page 9 for more information on creating your own combination of letters and designs. Remember to apply interlining before you start to stitch and neaten the fabric edges so they don't fray.

Stitch the letters and motifs following the instructions given and to complete stitch your name preferably, (initials will do) and the date of completion. This embroidery must not be ironed when it is completed, block following the directions given on page 11.

Threads DMC Coton a broder 16/Perle 8, unless otherwise stated Anne 602 Raspberry pink, stitching instructions for A are given on page 28. The other letters were stitched with as few stops and starts as possible to ensure a nice line to the embroidery. For example 'n' was stitched by working the curve first and adding the little top stroke last. As a general rule I stitch as I write but look at the letters you need to stitch and work out the way you feel will be easier. There are no hard and fast rules.

The following designs were stitched using the threads and following the instructions given with each design:
Caterpillar - page 58 with L, Bird - page 38 with F, Daisy Flower - page 58 with L, Pear - page 86 with Z, Ladybird - page 86 with Z, Sheep - page 32 with C, Fish - page 78 with V, Mushroom - page 62 with N, Bee - page 64 with O, Bell flower - page 60 with M, Grapes and leaf - page 40 with G, Umbrella - page 60 with M.
Cornflower page 42 with H using 502, 3713 and 3689.
Blossom - This flower is stitched following the instructions given on page 46 but using yellow 743 to work the chain stitch outline of each petal and lemon 744 to fill each petal. The straight stitch between each petal is worked in lemon and a small pearl bead is sewn at the end of each straight stitch with a large pearl bead sewn at the centre of the blossom. The stem is worked in chain stitch using olive green 469. Perle 8 or coton a broder 16 was used throughout.

MAKING UP

After stitching a design as special as this, the finish is extremely important. The heavier fabric I used made this a little more challenging! Make sure the design is on the right hand side and centred. Trim your cover to allow 12cm (4 3/4") at each end for pockets and 1cm (3/8") top and bottom.

Turn under flap edge of pocket to neaten and then turn flap edges inside to form pockets. Pin or tack in place and check the cover fits your book when closed! For a nice finished effect this fit needs to be tight. Adjust fit as required.

Cut two small pieces of fine fabric for facing the spine edges, pin or tack in place and then stitch 1cm (5/8") right across the top and bottom including the spine facing.

Turn the cover right side out, fold under the raw edge of the spine facings and catch down by hand to the inside of the cover. Slip your book inside the cover and it is ready to use and be admired!

Wrong side

Turn under raw edges of pocket flaps to neaten

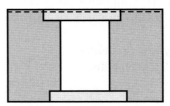

Turn in flaps to form pockets and attach two strips of fine fabric for facing the spine then sew across the top and bottom

BABY & SMALL DESIGNS

These are all simple designs to enjoy and give pleasure in the doing and receiving. Every piece of embroidery does not have to be a time consuming masterpiece. I really enjoy doing these little things and hope you do too. I make many cards, for family, special friends, on anniversaries, any and all of the special occasions that my family and friends celebrate. The designs can of course be taken out of the cards after they have been received and framed, used on the tops of little boxes, made into pin cushions etc. The same small designs work well on babies bibs, box tops, and the lids of china bowls. The possibilities are limitless. Instructions are given here for just a few different designs I do hope they will inspire you to make your own!

REQUIREMENTS
- If making a card, purchase cards of the shape, size and colour you desire from your local needlework supplier purchase first so that you know the space available for your embroidery
- China bowl - again purchase first so that you know the space available for your embroidery
- Choose a firm, closely-woven cream fabric such as crewel linen or similar good quality fabric to fit the cards or item for which the embroidery is intended
- Iron on backing fabric 'stayflex' or similar
- Crewel No 8 and Tapestry 22-26 Needles

Trace the designs you select and transfer to your fabric. See page 10 for more information on transferring a design and page 9 for more information on creating your own designs. Remember to apply interlining before you start to stitch.

CHINA BOWL LID - **refer to colour photograph page 52**
I am very fond of raspberries and the rich variety of colours that can be used to embroider them. I stitched these two so that their green sepals would tone with the green bowl. The bowl would look very attractive on anyone's dressing table and is the perfect place for holding earrings or other little treasures.

When you have bought a bowl, box lid or frame, determine the space available for your design and then choose motifs that will fit, the motifs can of course be enlarged or reduced as required and if you feel your drawing skills are a little limited go to your local photocopy shop!

The raspberries were stitched using the threads and following the instructions given on page 84 for 'ready to eat' and 'almost ripe' raspberries. On completion I sewed a few green seed beads over the surface of the linen, laced the embroidery over card, stitched a little backing in place and fitted the lid inside the lid frame.

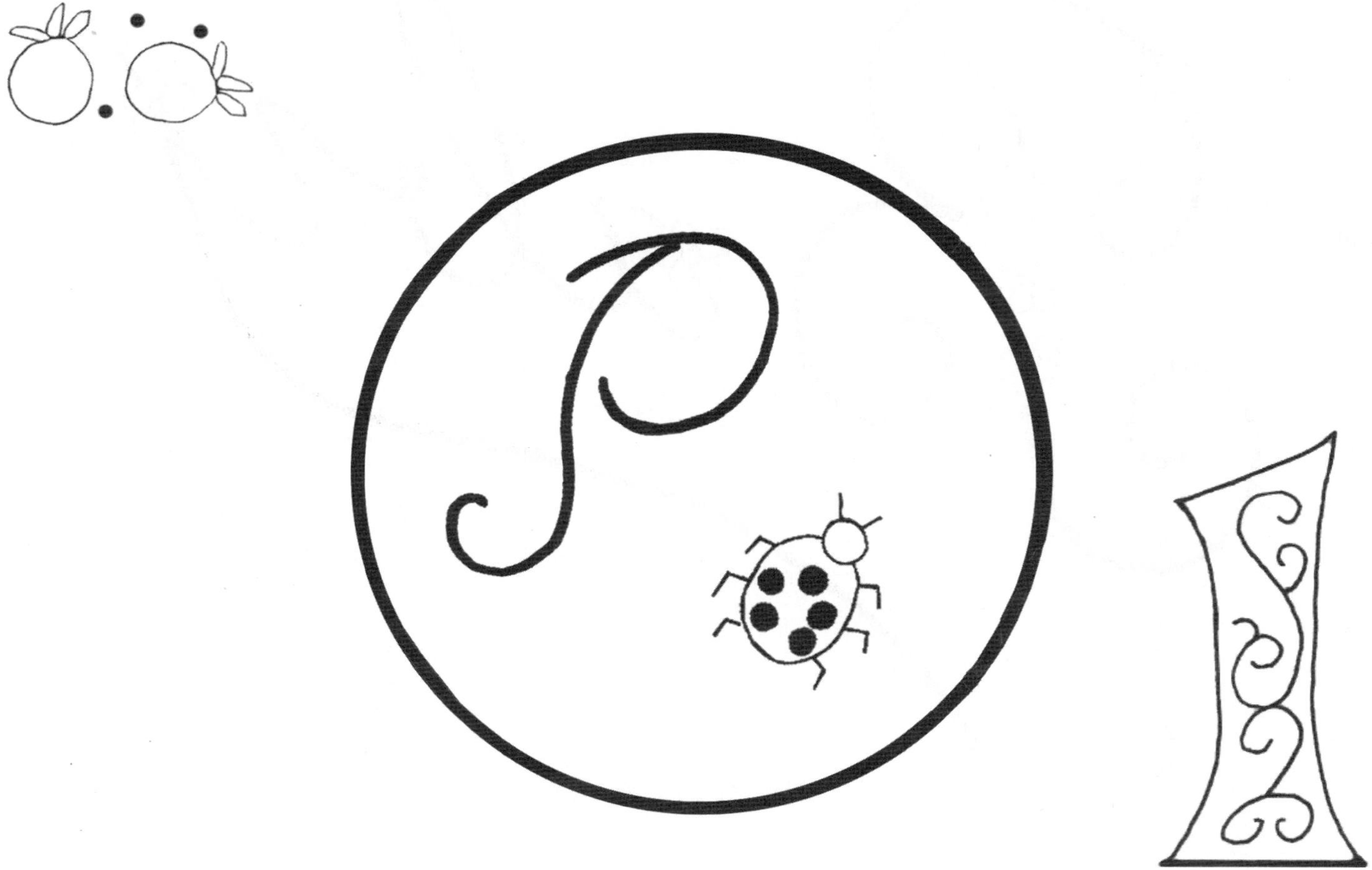

'P' BIRTHDAY CARD AND BIB

Refer to the colour photograph on page 50 for additional detail

Stitch the letters following the instructions given with the appropriate letter. The lady bird was stitched following the instructions given on page 86 with 'Z'. To give the letter more emphasis I outlined the letter and ladybird with a ladder stitched circle. The letter was stitched using 904 apple green and the circle was stitched using 336 dark blue. If you wish to use a different sized circle - use a plate or cup to get the size you want. On the card I sewed red seed beads over the background to give it more interest.

To put the embroidery in the card you may wish to staple it to a firm cardboard backing or glue it. Whilst glue is not usually recommended for embroidery I make these quickly and don't expect them to last for posterity!

NUMBER 1 BIRTHDAY CARD see page 53

Trace the outline given and work in ladder stitch using 321 bright red. The scrolling design inside the number was worked in chain stitch using gold metallic thread. Sew a sprinkling of gold beads to the background and your card is complete! Attach to a cardboard backing in your preferred method.

SHEET see page 53

Turn a simple white linen or cotton sheet into luxurious bedding with the addition of 'Baby' stitched in blue with simple little yellow flowers for decoration. It is another way to say 'welcome' to a new baby and will look very special in its cot.

REQUIREMENTS
- One bought cot sheet
- Crewel No 8 needle
- DMC Perle 8 or Coton a broder 16 799 medium blue
- DMC 744 lemon and 743 yellow stranded cotton

Trace the design on page 101 onto the cot sheet and embroider in ladder stitch using medium blue.
If you wish to embroider different shapes, allow for these. Do not carry the thread across the break in stitching as it is likely to cause puckers in your finished work, rather stop, finish the thread then restart on the other side of the break.

The yellow forget-me-nots are stitched following the instructions on page 28 with 'A' but using one thread of lemon to outline the petals in chain stitch, still using the same thread fill each petal with detached buttonhole stitch. Use two threads of yellow to make a French knot for the centre of the flower.

DO NOT USE ANY BEADS, OR OTHER EMBELLISHMENTS ON ANY BABY GARMENTS.

W - FROG WITH BULRUSHES

Refer to the colour photograph of 'W' on page 51 for additional detail

A charming design makes an everyday creature into a unique personal treasure. This lifelike frog is ready to jump into any little boy (or girl's) room! Embroider your son or grandson's initial and 'freddy frog' for his next birthday, you could personalise it further with the addition of his birth date.

REQUIREMENTS
• Choose a firm, closely-woven cream fabric such as crewel linen or similar good quality fabric - 25 cm.sq. - 25 cm sq.
• Iron on backing fabric 'stayflex' or similar - 25 cm sq.
• Crewel No 8 and Tapestry 22-26 Needles

Trace the design given on page 80 change the letter if necessary and transfer it to your fabric. See page 10 for more information on transferring a design and page 9 for more information on creating your own letters design. Remember to apply interlining before you start to stitch.

Stitch the initial and motif following the instructions given below. Your embroidery is not complete without the addition of your name preferably (initials will do) and the date of completion - these do not have to be seen but should be somewhere! This embroidery must not be ironed when it is completed, block following the directions given on page 11 and then take it to your favourite framer. Wait for the recipient's delight.

THREADS - DMC Coton a broder 16/Perle 8, unless otherwise stated

W - see stitching instructions 'W'
815   dark ruby red

Stitch the Frog, bulrushes and stones using the threads and following the instructions given on page 80.